# Condo Buying & Ownership Made Simple:

## Tips to Save Time and Money

# DISCLAIMER

This work is designed to provide accurate and authoritative information regarding the subject matter covered. We assume no liability for any consequences arising from the use of the information contained in the book. Information offered here is provided strictly as a general guideline. Neither the author nor the publisher renders investment, accounting, legal, or other professional services. The completeness of the information and the opinions contained herein cannot be guaranteed.

# DEDICATION

"Whatever you do, do all to the glory of God."

1 Corinthians 10:31

It was my husband's idea to write this book. Jim has lovingly encouraged and supported me in doing so.

# AUTHOR'S BIO

## THE PROPOSAL

I spent 25 years in Administrative Management in corporate America. I retired at the same time that my husband and I decided to downsize and move into a condominium. The "Introduction" talks about my wild and crazy experience serving on the Board of Directors for our association. It also tells about the early stage of my community association management business.

When I began managing condominiums on a part-time basis, I also began to accumulate files of resources. Contractors, attorneys, accountants, and title companies were the primary ones. I also created forms for *everything*! My years of experience in administration were really paying off.

One spring day, my phone rang. It was an attorney I had met through managing one of the condominium associations. He informed me there was a condominium management company in my county that was up for sale and that he knew the owner. He thought I should buy it and become a full-time management company. He stated our area was in urgent need of a *good* one. My first response was, "Why would I want to *buy* a management company when I already had my own?" He asked me to meet him for lunch to discuss the idea. I came away from that lunch *a little bit* convinced that it might be a good idea. He gave me the name and phone number of the seller. There were a number of pros and cons to consider.

A couple of months later, the seller called me and stated her attorney friend told her I might be interested in buying her management company. (I guess he **really** wanted me to do this!) I told her I wasn't sure if I was interested. She convinced me to meet with her to discuss terms. We met a couple of times and reached an agreement. That was in 1997. I incorporated my company, opened an office, and began to work full time. The business grew by leaps and bounds just through word of mouth. I spent nothing on advertising and promotion.

## BACK TO SCHOOL

My company joined Community Associations Institute (CAI), a nonprofit association created in 1973 to educate and represent condominium associations, homeowner associations, and cooperatives. It is the first and only nationwide organization created solely to educate and certify community association managers and to help consumers identify managers who have demonstrated competency and knowledge in this profession.

As a result of successfully completing many hours of education, CAI awarded me the following **designations**. CAI also requires continuing education in order to maintain these credentials.

- *CMCA® (Certified Manager of Community Associations)*
- *AMS® (Association Management Specialist)*

My education through CAI gave me **certification** in the following areas of community association management:

- *The Essentials of Community Association Management*
- *Facilities Management*
- *Association Communications*

- *Community Governance*
- *Risk Management*
- *Financial Management*

When I retired from this second career after 17 years, I told my husband it was a shame that all of my knowledge and experience was no longer going to be of value. He said, "Why don't you write a book?" I thought it was a *grand* idea. Because of my involvement in community associations for so many years, as a unit owner, board president, and condominium management company professional, **_I understand the problems and concerns of buyers, owners, board members and management companies_**.

Through this book and my website, I pass on my expertise and experience to buyers and owners.

www.condo-condominium.com

# TABLE OF CONTENTS

# INTRODUCTION

*Why should you read this book before you buy a condo?*

This book will inform buyers of condominiums about the obligations of condominium living <u>before</u> they sign on the dotted line.

*Why should you read this book if you already own a condo?*

Owners of condos will discover how to live happily in a community association and how to bring about change in a non-threatening manner.

*Unit owners have many more good stories than bad of their experiences living in condominium associations. My story is a bad one that turned into a wonderful career!*

*My husband and I had decided it was time to downsize from our home to a condominium. We didn't want to worry any more about maintenance, landscaping, and snow removal. We were so excited that we had found a beautiful condo on a golf course and it was being sold from an estate—so we got it at a lower than normal price. However, there were problems of which we were not aware.*

## MY HORRID EXPERIENCE!

It was the day after Thanksgiving—moving day! The moving van had been gone for a couple of hours when the phone rang. I answered it to hear, "My name is — — and *I'm calling to let you know you can't park in your driveway.*" "*WHAT?!*" I questioned. "Well, it says so in the governing documents," she responded. I asked her what she meant by the governing documents, and she said, "You know, the Declaration and Bylaws." No, I didn't know. I explained to her that there were four cars in the family—two for us and two for our young adult children. How in the world could this have happened? I was totally confused and angry. Why didn't someone tell us about this before we bought the unit? Why didn't our realtor know the rules for the community? Why didn't the title company provide us with the governing documents before the deal closed? Why didn't someone tell us these documents even existed?! I was furious!

During the rest of the conversation, the caller proceeded to advise me there were many rules that all who live in this community association must obey. These "restrictions" were in the "governing documents." The caller continued, "Haven't you read them?" "Read them?!" I responded in frustration. I reiterated that I didn't know what governing documents were or that they even existed! She informed me she was president of the Board of Directors and she would drop off a set of them to me that evening.

In the meantime, my children had to park far away at the opposite end of the condominium property because the developer had not constructed guest parking anywhere in the community. I couldn't have been more unhappy, nor could they. They both had after-school jobs at local fast food restaurants and it was usually dark when they arrived home. We were <u>very</u> concerned for their safety!

## LEGAL DOCUMENTS

I spent that night reading this big stack of papers (several times), written of course in legalese—Declaration of Condominium Ownership, Bylaws, Amendments to the Declaration of Condominium Ownership. They were difficult to understand, but in the "Restrictions as to Use and Occupancy of Condominium Property" section, it stated, "Parking of vehicles in driveways is prohibited." And that wasn't all! There were other restrictions—some logical and some not! We didn't realize we had moved into a "police state."

I telephoned the board president the next day to ask how we could get a waiver because of the four cars in our family. For that matter, how could restrictions be changed? She said I would have to present my questions to the Board of Directors in writing and at a meeting. She went on to say that was only the starting point because the board didn't have the authority to change the Declaration and Bylaws. "So how could changes be made?" I asked. "Just come to the meeting and you'll find out!" she responded rudely.

She informed me there would be a board meeting on the following Thursday at her unit, but that all requests must be submitted in writing prior to the meeting. All the board members would be given a copy of my request. The day was spent composing what I hoped would be an acceptable, polite appeal for a waiver of the rule because of my two children and guests we would have in the future. "How could anyone survive in here with these parking rules? Surely I'm not the only one with a problem," I thought.

I finally got a phone call the night before the meeting, telling me the board had approved hearing me and that I was scheduled to speak after the board completed its business session. The night finally came, and it was my turn. I calmly presented my situation, taking great pains to touch their hearts about my children's parking situation. The board president stated that, in order to change the parking rules, it would require a vote of the entire ownership of the association. "Why?" I asked. "Because that's what the Declaration says," she said as she pointed to the specific page on which that was stated. "Didn't you read the papers I gave you?" she asked. Of course I had, but hadn't really understood all the legal language. She continued by telling me they had tried to pass other changes, but the owners never wanted any of them. "After all, it's their community, so it's their decision!" she stated triumphantly.

I returned home in tears. How could we live with this? There was no way out—we would lose our shirts if we sold the unit immediately. What could we do? We decided I should try to get elected to the Board of Directors as a start.

## BIRTH OF A NEW CAREER

I continued to attend board meetings. Usually I was the only owner, other than the board members, in attendance. One of the members became ill and had to resign; the rest of the board (except for the president!) asked me to finish out his term (one more year). I agreed with delight. Thus began my career in community associations! I was elected as the board president two months later and spent six years serving on the board. The prior president did not get re-elected at the next annual meeting, but I did! By the way, this was a "self-managed" association; the board members did all the work.

During that time, we convinced the ownership to pass several Amendments to the Declaration. Guess which one was first! After the parking issue was resolved, we had other issues:

- The prior president had a dog that she allowed to run free on the property, in violation of the rule that all pets must be leashed. We sent her violation letters and threatened to fine her, but to no avail. I guess she thought she was untouchable due to her prior position! However, her dog made the mistake of biting one of the children in the community. Then she allowed the dog to bite the child again, despite several warnings! For-

tunately, the child was okay. We had the dog removed
from the property (much to her amazement).

- Then there was the owner who asked permission to
make a modification to his rear patio area. We requested he present his plan at the next board meeting.
He came to the meeting with a professionally drawn
layout of his proposed changes. They were massive—
so extensive they were going to cost him $23,000! We
voted to deny his request. There were two reasons for
the denial: 1) his unit would become completely different than all the other units and 2) he would be attach-
ing patio walls to the exterior of the building. *He
started construction anyway!* We continued to warn
him in writing to stop, but he continued to completion.
We filed a lawsuit to force him to remove everything
and won. It cost him another bundle to restore the
area to its original condition.

- Water was infiltrating the basements of several of the
units in one of our buildings. After hiring a civil engi-
neer, he reported the building had been constructed
below grade and would need to be raised up one foot.
Wow! No one on the board had the expertise to handle
this job. But necessity is the mother of invention. We
hired a contractor to do the work and the civil engi-
neer who'd made the report oversaw the work. Fortu-
nately, the outcome was excellent, but it took months
to complete and cost more than $30,000! We had been
very frugal with the association's money, so we were
able to complete the project without a special assessment to all the owners.

By this time (three years had passed), we were getting very
tired of all the work. We decided to hire a management company and formed a committee to research and evaluate all of the

companies in our area. They narrowed the search down to two. We interviewed both and hired the one we thought was best.

We employed the management company for two years. They used us as a "training ground," changing the assigned property manager six times! We fired them. As the board met in my unit's livingroom, we all looked at each other and said, "Now what do we do?" We had researched all the management companies in the area and didn't like any of the others. The board asked me to become the property manager. I agreed (I'd been doing most of the work anyway). I resigned from the board so as not to have a conflict of interest.

Thus began my management career—from the basement of my condo. By the way, I did make sure that doing business from my condo was NOT against the Declaration!

I managed the association for several years and took on a few more—working at home was wonderful. As I became acquainted with the owners at the different complexes, I found my "moving in" story was not unusual. Most people who purchase a condominium have no idea what association living really means. I found myself spending an enormous amount of time educating the owners.

My desire is to prevent others from making unnecessary mistakes due to lack of knowledge. I hope you will see my heart as you read this book.

---

*You've found your dream condo and you can't wait to move in!*

*So you decide, even though you haven't read the association's documents, that everything will be okay and the rules just can't be that bad. Your assumption may not be correct! You <u>must</u> know what the rules are. Only then will you be able to decide if you can live by them.*

> **PLEASE, PLEASE** *take the time to do your research!*
>
> *Read all of the association's governing documents and rules before you make any decision. Also, be sure to have the financial condition reviewed. You don't want to find yourself suddenly responsible for years of poor financial planning on the part of a mismanaged association.*
>
> *When an association board acts in a responsible manner and makes good business decisions and when the owners and residents know the rules and follow them, community associations become wonderful places in which to live. They offer a wide range of lifestyles that suit people of all ages and interests.*

## WHAT'S IN THIS BOOK FOR THE CONDO BUYER?

>>> You will be _confident_ about your decision to purchase a condo and be _familiar_ with the association, even before you move in!

### OR

>>> You will decide _not_ to live in a condo, based on the facts, and conclude that association living is not for you!

## WHAT'S IN THIS BOOK FOR THE CONDO OWNER?

>>> *You will discover how to live harmoniously in a community association and how to produce changes you believe are necessary.*

# WHAT IS THE DIFFERENCE BETWEEN A CONDOMINIUM ASSOCIATION AND A HOMEOWNERS' ASSOCIATION?

*Be sure you understand the real estate lingo!*
The definitions of types of community associations define owner-ship, not architectural style.

Joe and Mary moved into their dream condo—at least they <u>thought</u> it was a condo. A few months after they moved in, they noticed a small hole in the siding on the back of the unit. They placed a call to the property manager to request it be fixed. After all, the exteriors of units in condominiums are the association's responsibility. The manager told them the repair was Joe and Mary's responsibility. They couldn't believe it! Joe wrote a letter to the Board of Directors to report the manager's mistaken information. Much to their chagrin, they received a response that the complex was a planned community, not a condominium, and to check the Declaration they received when they moved in. Sure enough, the Declaration stated it was a planned community association. But everything <u>seemed</u> the same as a condo when they were looking to buy! If they had known they would be responsible for the exterior surfaces of their unit, they wouldn't have purchased it.

## DEFINITIONS

There are actually, by definition, three (3) types of residential community associations:

1. Condominium

In a condominium, the individual owns:

- His or her living unit and
- An undivided interest in the common elements and facilities of the association.

 *Buyer's Tip—The condominium association owns no real estate.*

2. Planned Community (Homeowners' Association or HOA)

In a planned community, the individual owns:

- His or her lot and/or living unit.

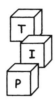

*Buyer's Tip—The homeowners' association owns the common elements and facilities.*

3. Cooperative

In a cooperative, the individual:

- Owns stock or membership in the cooperative and
- Holds a proprietary lease or occupancy agreement for his or her living unit.

*Buyer's Tip—The cooperative association owns all real estate, including the units.*

## GOVERNANCE

Q  DO CONDOMINIUMS AND HOMEOWNERS' ASSOCI-
ATIONS HAVE THE SAME TYPES OF GOVERNING
DOCUMENTS?

A  Some are the same. (We will not discuss cooperatives
here—there are not many of them and they may
disappear altogether over time.)

|  | Condominiums | HOAs |
| --- | :---: | :---: |
| Governed by General State Statutes | X | X |
| Governed by Specific State Statutes | X |  |
| Are Defined as Planned Communities |  | X |
| Have a Declaration of Condominium Ownership | X |  |

|                                                             | Condominiums | HOAs |
| ----------------------------------------------------------- | :----------: | :--: |
| Have a Declaration of Covenants, Conditions, and Restrictions |              |  X   |
| Have Bylaws                                                 |      X       |  X   |
| Have Master Deed                                           |      X       |  X   |
| Have Articles of Incorporation (if incorporated)          |      X       |  X   |

## RESPONSIBILITIES

Q ARE OWNERS' RESPONSIBILITIES DIFFERENT IN CONDOMINIUMS AND HOMEOWNERS' ASSOCIATIONS?

A Yes, some are. Based on the definitions provided here, some of the responsibilities of the owners and the association will differ. Some of the differences are, but not limited to, the following:

|                                                        | Condominiums | HOAs        |
| ------------------------------------------------------ | :----------: | :---------: |
| Repair, maintenance, replacement of building exteriors |  Association |    Owner    |
| Landscaping and snow removal                           |  Association |    Owner    |
| Road repair and replacement                            |  Association | Local Gov't.|
| Exterior pest control                                  |  Association |    Owner    |

Q WHAT ARE THE SIMILARITIES BETWEEN CONDO-MINIUMS AND HOMEOWNERS' ASSOCIATIONS?

A Some of the similarities are:

• Both are not only communities, but businesses.

- There is a Board of Directors, which is elected annually by the membership.
- Both may have committees.
- There are Board of Directors' and owners' meetings.
- Both may have rules regarding conduct and architectural changes.
- Each has financial reporting requirements.
- The owner assessments (maintenance fees) are established by the budget.
- Both have bills to pay for the common services.
- Both may employ a management company or be self-managed.
- Each may or may not have recreational facilities.

> Do not define the types of community associations according to architectural style. There's always an exception!
>
> When talking to a realtor or lender, terms like "townhouse" or "cluster home" may be used, but be sure you know which of the three types of associations you are buying into so you know what you will or will not own!

 *WHAT'S NEXT? Now that you know the differences between the three types of residential community associations, we will turn our attention to condominiums.*

# WHAT IS A
# CONDOMINIUM?

Many owners end up confused and unhappy because they misunderstand what a condominium really is.

*Be an informed condo owner!*

A popular radio show host says he didn't know what an association was when he moved into a condominium. He thought it was great that he paid the dues and someone else collected the trash and shoveled the snow. After he moved in, he decided it was much more than that. A home buyer in Florida called in to the show complaining about the "typical deal in Florida," where a home buyer doesn't get the association's governing documents until settlement. If you're like most people, you don't have time to read them. You're signing so many other documents. Why on earth is that stuff not given to you until closing? The radio host states that the documents are for anyone and everyone who lives in an association. His listeners shouldn't be bashful about asking for a copy——before they buy.

Q WHAT IS THE ACTUAL DEFINITION OF A COMMU-
  NITY ASSOCIATION (CONDOMINIUM)?

A A community association is a group of owners who wish to
  provide a communal basis for preserving, maintaining,

and enhancing their homes and property. It is a type of joint ownership of real property in which portions of the property are commonly owned and other portions are individually owned.

- Membership is mandatory and automatic for all owners.
- Legal documents, such as the *Declaration and Bylaws*, mutually bind all owners.
- Mandatory, lien-based economic charges (called assessments or maintenance fees) are levied on each owner in order to operate and maintain the condominium association.
- A community association is a business.
- Use and enjoyment of the property are for all owners.

## SOME AREAS OF CONFUSION REGARDING CONDOMINIUM LIVING

- It is NOT a democracy!
- It is NOT a social organization!
- It is NOT a dictatorship or monarchy!

Q  WHAT IS THE DIFFERENCE BETWEEN LIVING IN A SINGLE-FAMILY HOME AND A CONDOMINIUM UNIT?

A  <u>Maintenance and Replacement</u>

### Single-Family Home:

- *You must personally perform or hire someone to perform all maintenance and repair work.*

- *You pay directly for all work performed.*
- *You make your own choices of styles, materials, colors, etc. for the entire property.*
- *You establish your own budget and replacement (reserve) fund.*

## Condominium Unit:

- *You <u>usually</u> don't perform exterior maintenance personally.*
- *You pay assessments (maintenance fees) and/or special assessments to the association for repairs and/or replacements.*
- *You have choices of style, materials, colors, etc. for **only** the interior of your unit.*
- *You don't set the budget—the Board of Directors establishes the budget and replacement (reserve) fund.*

## A  <u>Lifestyle</u>

## Single-Family Home:

- *Restrictions are set by local, state, and federal government agencies.*
- *Social freedom—you set your own "house rules."*

## Condominium Unit:

- *Restrictions are set by local, state, and federal government agencies.*
- *Secondary restrictions are also set by the condominium's governing documents and by the Board of Directors.*

## Q  WHAT ARE SOME OF THE BENEFITS OF LIVING IN A CONDOMINIUM?

The association normally does the exterior work.

- Landscaping, fertilization, snow removal, pest control, etc.
- Maintenance of the building exteriors
- Maintenance of the common roads, driveways, walkways
- Provision for and maintenance of recreational facilities

The Board of Directors makes most of the decisions.

- Planned social activities
- Dispute resolution when owners infringe on each other's rights
- Safety of owners and residents by installation of safety systems and procedures

The association collects the assessments (maintenance fees) and pays for the services.

- This is similar to "budget billing."
- Assessments (maintenance fees) are for operating, maintenance, and replacement expenses.

---

There are similarities and differences between single-family living and community association living. Those differences are VERY important and this book is dedicated to explaining them!

---

 *WHAT'S NEXT? Now let's talk about the advantages and disadvantages of living in a community association.*

# WHY LIVE IN A CONDOMINIUM?

Every time you drive down the freeway in big cities, near suburbs, resort areas, or small towns, you see condominium developments sprouting up. They come in all sizes and shapes—large high-rises, smaller low-rises, contemporary cubes, Mediterranean villas, sprawling ranch-style developments—luxury versions, low cost models, and those in between.

**What makes condominiums so popular?**

According to Alexandria, Virginia-based Community Associations Institute, an estimated one in six Americans lives in an association-managed community. Planned communities account for 50 to 55 percent of this total, condominiums 40 to 45 percent, and cooperatives 5 to 7 percent. Community associations have become popular because they help protect home values, provide affordable ownership opportunities, and promote efficient land planning.

## ADVANTAGES

- In our fluctuating economy, owning your own living quarters is a wise investment. Why pay rent when you can be building equity in a home?
- Interest on your mortgage loan may be an allowable income tax deduction.

- You can enjoy freedom from performing exterior maintenance that is not available in a separate, traditional residence.
- Someone else is responsible for the landscaping, snow removal, and maintenance of the building exteriors. This is a big plus for non-do-it-yourselfers, busy professionals, on-the-go young people, and senior citizens.
- The cost of recreational facilities is shared. Therefore, many condominiums offer swimming pools, exercise facilities, party rooms, tennis courts, golf courses, and other luxuries that you may not be able to afford on your own.
- If you have a disagreement with your neighbor, a dispute resolution process is available.
- Security systems are "built in." Because of the proximity of your neighbors, when you take a vacation, just lock your door and go!
- Often, there are organized social activities for all ages and occasions.
- You may have a voice in the management by offering your services to the Board of Directors or special committees.
- Property values normally increase because condominium living is a very popular lifestyle and the association makes sure the property's appearance is professionally maintained and consistent throughout.
- Young adult professionals, empty-nesters, and seniors who are in good health generally thrive.

## DISADVANTAGES

- It is a much different lifestyle than usual and takes some "getting used to."

- Because of the proximity in which you live to others, there can be disagreements.
- You are bound by rules established by the association for the benefit of all owners.
- You may not have any control over the assessments (maintenance fees) charged by the association to all owners every year.
- The Board of Directors controls colors of the building exteriors, styles and colors of exterior lights, windows and doors, and choices of landscape plantings.
- Some condominiums lack recreational facilities for children and teens.
- Parking may be limited or not convenient.
- Those who are handicapped may have difficulty navigating the environment.

> *There are wonderful advantages to living in a condominium. There are also disadvantages.*
> ***Make sure you know what they are!***

 *WHAT'S NEXT? What do you need to know about the differences between a new unit and a resale unit? Does the developer do more than just build condominiums?*

# SHOULD I PURCHASE NEW INSTEAD OF A RESALE?

There is nothing quite like living where no one has lived before. Everything is spotless and fresh. Newly constructed units also tempt purchasers because they usually have the latest designs and features. In most cases, the purchaser can select interior components, i.e., appliances and floor coverings.

***But can there be problems?***

A businessman who gives financial seminars headed up a committee to transfer control of a homeowners' association from the developer to the homeowners. He stated that the transition from developer control to homeowner control isn't easy. Some attorneys say that developers don't want a community to turn around and change things that might impact sales. Associations could forbid construction trucks or put limits on pets or a lot of other things that might hurt construction or slow down sales. Homeowners often may not be prepared for the immense responsibility and expense that running a new community entails. Running an association can be similar to running a business, with fees for insurance, management, and maintenance. Therefore, taking control of a development requires financial and legal expertise that communities that choose not to hire a management company might lack. Developers sometimes keep home-owners' association fees artificially low while they are in control. Once the homeowners take over, they find that the costs of maintaining the community are much higher than they are accustomed to paying.

## FACTS ABOUT THE DECLARANT (DEVELOPER)

Transition of control from the declarant to the unit owners is governed by state law. In a new development, there are different levels of declarant involvement, and that involvement changes as units are sold. Initially, the declarant holds all seats on the Board of Directors. When declarant representatives sit as members of the board, they have a fiduciary duty to take action that is in the association's best interest, even if it is detrimental to the declar-ant. As units are sold, the declarant has fewer seats on board, based on conveyance of a set percentage of units.

State law also requires that transfer to the owners occurs no later than a set number of years following the sale of the initial unit.

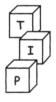

*Buyer's Tip—If the declarant reserved the right to expand the condominium in the future, that provision would be found in the Declaration. It is important to find out if expansion is planned so you will know <u>how many additional units</u> may be added. You will also want to know <u>when</u> the expansion period ends.*

## ADVANTAGES OF BUYING NEW:

- *The declarant may not have to pay real estate com-mission, so the unit may be less expensive.*

- *You get a warranty on the construction of the unit for a specified period of time.*
- *If you buy for a reduced price and the development is successful, your investment may appreciate quickly.*
- *Owner assessments (maintenance fees) may be low because there is no track record on which to base the budget.*

## RISKS OF BUYING NEW:

- *If you buy into a new complex that is not complete, there is no assurance that the declarant will finish the project.*
- *Sometimes declarants are poor planners. They may have thought they could complete the project for a certain amount of money, only to discover, part way through the process, that they can't.*
- *Some declarants go bankrupt and the project stalls.*
- *Sometimes declarants abandon a project. Sales may not be as strong as expected, so the units don't sell as quickly, forcing the declarant to fold.*
- *Owner assessments are set based on a certain number of units. If only half that number are completed and sold, owner costs could be much higher.*
- *If any of these events occurs, the complex may develop a bad reputation, and you may not be able to get out without a significant financial loss.*
- *If you cannot sell your unit, you may be trapped there for years in a partially completed project.*
- *Lawsuits may be filed against the declarant. As a result, the declarant may be exonerated or go bankrupt, leaving problems unresolved.*

- *Units built today are frequently not constructed with the same quality of materials as those used in past decades.*
- *It can take years for construction problems to surface.*
- *"Glitches" left unfinished by a construction contractor may not appear immediately.*
- *You may not be able to view the unit you are buying. The purchase may have to be made based on viewing drawings or a model suite.*
- *There may be no replacement funds available because there may not have been enough time to set reserves aside.*

## THE DECLARANT'S (DEVELOPER'S) DISCLOSURE PACKAGE

A complete disclosure package normally includes:

- Offer to Purchase and Specifications
- Proposed Operating Budget and Fee Schedule
- Proposed Declaration and Bylaws
- Proposed Management Contract
- Proposed Site Plan
- Unit Layouts and Descriptions
- Warranty Programs

*Buying new may or may not be profitable.*

If the community is at least ten (10) years old, there is a track record of assessments and board meetings you can consider. Through asking questions, you should know the condition of the buildings.

You really don't know if a new development will be successful or how long it will take to sell all the units. However, if you have done your homework in checking out the declarant's track record and like the advantages of buying new, you will probably be happy.

*There are pros and cons to purchasing old and new. If you weigh them carefully, you can minimize your concerns and maximize your enjoyment.*

 *WHAT'S NEXT? You may now have more questions than you had before! The next chapter is filled with frequently asked questions.*

# FREQUENTLY ASKED
## QUESTIONS

You may be wondering which questions you should ask before you buy a condominium.

***HERE ARE ANSWERS TO SOME
OF THE MOST COMMON QUESTIONS.***

The heart of the community association lifestyle is based on owners cooperating with each other and volunteering to take turns serving on the Board of Directors. What is best for the entire community should become the prevailing attitude. The foundations of a successful association are common sense and individual rights giving way to the best interest of the community.

There are many references to the Declaration and Rules in this chapter. The definitions and purposes of the Declaration, Bylaws, Amendments and Rules are included in this book. See the Table of Contents for those specific chapters.

## ACCORDING TO THE RULES

Q  ARE PETS PERMITTED?

A  There may be limitations on pets. If so, the issue will be addressed in the "Restrictions" section of the

*Declaration*, usually under the heading of "Animals and Pets." There may also be a *Declaration Amendment* regarding pets. There most certainly will be rules governing pets.

**Q  CAN I OPERATE A BUSINESS OUT OF MY CONDO?**

A  The *Declaration* will state whether a business may be operated in the "Restrictions" section, usually under the heading of "Purpose of Property." Check also for *Declaration Amendments*. Get approval <u>before</u> running a business from your unit.

**Q  DO I HAVE TO CARRY INSURANCE ON MY CONDO?**

A  Yes, each should carry insurance that covers portions of the unit for which the owner is responsible, including any unit improvements or additions, personal property, and personal liability. The association purchases a master policy for the common property in accordance with the *Declaration* requirements. Your insurance agent should review the *Declaration* and *Bylaws* and also talk to the association's insurance agent. You may want to consider buying your insurance from the same agent/company that insures the association.

**Q  ARE SATELLITE DISHES PERMITTED?**

A  You usually may have a dish as long as it is not installed on any of the common elements. You should submit a drawing to the Board of Directors indicating the proposed location, height, and screening materials to be used. In many cases, the association has installed common satellite service that is available to all owners. If this is the case, individual dishes are normally prohibited.

Q MAY I LEASE OR SUB-LEASE MY UNIT?

A The *Declaration* and/or an *Amendment* will state the basis upon which you may lease your unit. If leasing is permitted, there will be some guidelines you must follow, such as: a) the unit may not be leased for hotel or transient purposes, b) owner must make the tenant aware of the association's rules, c) owner will be responsible for tenant violations and damages, and d) the lease document must contain a clause making it subject to the covenants and restrictions in the *Declaration, Bylaws, Amendments* and rules. In order for the association to **prohibit** leasing, it must be clearly stated in either the *Declaration* or a *Declaration Amendment.*

Q ARE "RENT" OR "SALE" SIGNS PERMITTED?

A Most associations have strict guidelines regarding signage. The *Declaration* and rules will cover them. Size, location, and times of display of signs should be clearly defined.

Q HOW MANY UNITS ARE RENTED?

A The percentage of units rented may influence whether lending institutions are willing to carry a mortgage. They may have specific guidelines to follow, some set by government entities. It is important to find out the percentage of the total units that are rented.

Q IS THERE AN AGE RESTRICTION?

A An age restriction requires that anyone living in the association be of a certain age. *Confirm that the restriction is valid.* Some complexes advertise they are for mature adults, but the governing documents do not actually have a section on this issue.

Q  IS THE PROPERTY USER-FRIENDLY FOR THE
   HANDICAPPED?

A  Hallway sizes, handrails, and ramps are extremely
   important for the handicapped. The structure of
   shower stalls and countertop heights are critical.
   Another consideration is whether you can have living
   assistance, either temporarily or permanently. Some
   age-restricted properties might not allow a younger
   person to live with you, even if they are providing
   health care.

Q  MAY I HAVE AN AIR CONDITIONING UNIT?

A  Frequently, the *Declaration* will so state. Most
   developers install central air. In older complexes, window
   air conditioners may or may not be permitted.

Q  WHEN CAN THE ASSOCIATION ENTER MY UNIT?

A  The *Declaration* may specify when the association has the
   right (easement) to enter your unit. For routine or
   scheduled maintenance, they should provide you with at
   least a 24-hour notice. In case of an emergency, such as a
   fire, they would enter without notice or break in if you
   weren't home.

Q  WHAT IF THE DECLARANT (DEVELOPER) IS STILL
   IN CONTROL?

A  If the declarant still holds the majority of seats on
   the Board of Directors, he will carry the most weight
   when voting on issues. It is also important to find out
   how many units are sold and how many are left to
   sell. This will tell you when the declarant's control
   will end.

Q IS THERE A PROBLEM IF THE DECLARANT (DEVELOPER) IS STILL IN CONTROL?

A Maybe. As long as the declarant in control, he or she makes all the decisions affecting the property. Some declarants (developers) are open to owner suggestions and some are not. Therefore, control by the declarant can be an advantage or a disadvantage.

Q ARE MEETINGS OF THE BOARD OF DIRECTORS OPEN FOR OWNERS TO ATTEND?

A Hopefully they are open. Attending meetings is a good way to find out what's happening on the property. Board meetings are also where decisions are made about maintenance, repair, and replacement of the common elements. These decisions affect your maintenance fees.

Q HOW DO I FIND OUT WHEN AND WHERE THE MEETINGS ARE HELD?

A Any member of the board will know when all the meetings are scheduled. Residents and the management company should also know. The schedule of meetings may be published in the association's newsletter.

Q ARE DECORATIONS PERMITTED ON THE EXTE-RIOR OF MY UNIT?

A The *Declaration* will state whether items may be attached to the exterior siding, doors, and windows of the unit. Generally, nothing of a permanent nature may be added. You will find this stated in the "Restrictions" section of the *Declaration*, usually under the heading of "Impairment of Structural Integrity of Building." However, the association may allow shrub bed decorations and/or lighting, doorknockers, flags, etc. by creating rules stating so.

Q  MAY I HAVE A GARAGE OR YARD SALE?

A  The *Declaration* may state this answer. Generally, there should be a rule covering this. Sometimes the association prohibits sales due to insurance restrictions.

Q  WHAT IF I WANT TO CHANGE THE STYLE AND COLOR OF WINDOWS AND DOORS?

A  If what you want to install is a change from what was originally in your unit, you will need permission from the Board of Directors to make the change. It is best to ask permission by supplying a picture to them of what you want, prior to installation. If you do not follow this procedure, you may be required to remove what you installed *at your own expense* and install the standard adopted by the association.

Q  ARE FLOWER BOXES, BIRD FEEDERS, AND SHRUB BED DECORATIONS PERMITTED?

A  There should be definite guidelines provided by the association regarding these items. Do not install any of the above without the prior consent of the Board of Directors or you may be subject to cost of removal and/or violation fees.

Q  IS THERE STORAGE SPACE INSIDE THE UNIT OR SOMEWHERE IN THE BUILDING?

A  Extra storage space inside the unit is preferable, but there may be assigned storage elsewhere on the property, such as a special room or floor in the building. You can learn this information in the *Declaration* or from the Board of Directors.

**Q WHAT ITEMS CAN BE PLACED ON THE BALCONY OR PATIO?**

A Some *Declarations* have a section that specifically states the items, including height and weight restrictions. Other *Declarations* are silent on the subject, but the board may have adopted a policy that would be covered in the rules. Many local government entities now have rules about barbecue grills.

**Q IS THIS A SECURE COMPLEX? MAY I INSTALL MY OWN SECURITY SYSTEM?**

A The property may be secured by an electronic system, there may be a security guard, or there may be no security at all. If there is no rule on individual security systems, you will need to request permission from the Board of Directors before installation.

**Q DOES CONDO LIVING MEAN NO WORK FOR ME?**

A This answer is found in the *Declaration*. The answer is somewhere between no work and lots of work. If you don't intend to volunteer for the Board of Directors or committees, the answer is probably no work. Obviously, the opposite is true if you volunteer your services. If the association has a management company, owner involvement can be greatly reduced. The other determining factor is what parts of the property you are expected to maintain. The amount of work you will be

required to do more or less depends on the particular
unit that you are purchasing.

Q IS THE NUMBER OF PEOPLE WHO CAN LIVE IN OR
VISIT THE UNIT RESTRICTED?

A The *Declaration* normally addresses this issue. The number
of people or families per residential unit may be stated.
There may also be restrictions on the number of visitors you
may have and how long they may stay temporarily in the
unit. There may be municipal ordinances that control the
number of occupants per unit.

## PARKING AND VEHICLES

Q MAY I PERFORM VEHICLE MAINTENANCE
ON THE PROPERTY?

A The *Declaration* may state this answer. Generally, only
small repairs may be done and they usually must be done
within the confines of your garage. If you have no garage,
you will probably not be able to make repairs within the
complex. If the *Declaration* doesn't address this, check
the rules.

Q I HAVE A CAMPER. AM I ALLOWED TO STORE IT
ON THE PROPERTY?

A Generally, the answer is "no" unless the association has a
specific location on the property for this type of storage.
The *Declaration* or an *Amendment* may state this answer.
If not, there should be a rule for it.

Q  I HAVE TO DRIVE MY COMPANY'S VEHICLE TO
   AND FROM WORK BECAUSE I'M ON CALL 24/7.
   WILL THIS BE A PROBLEM?

A  Some associations do not allow commercial vehicles to be
   parked on the property. There may also be restrictions
   on the size and weight of vehicles. Check the *Declaration*
   and the rules.

Q  WHAT ARE MY PARKING ARRANGEMENTS AS THE
   OWNER? WHAT ABOUT MY GUESTS?

A  Most complexes have at least one space per unit. It may
   be outside in a parking lot, in a separate building(s)
   with parking spaces, or in its own garage. Parking
   spaces may or may not be assigned. Parking facilities
   may be stated in the *Declaration* or the association
   may have parking rules. Be sure to find out where your
   guests can park and how long guest vehicles are
   permitted in any given area.

Q  MAY I PARK IN MY DRIVEWAY AND/OR ON THE
   STREET OVERNIGHT?

A  The *Declaration* may address this issue. The association
   may have rules about both. There may also be a
   municipal ordinance regarding street parking.

Q  WHAT IF I NEED MORE PARKING SPACES THAN
   ARE ASSIGNED TO THE UNIT?

A  Frankly speaking, you shouldn't move into a property
   that has more limits than you can tolerate, whether it's
   for parking or for any other reason!

Q  HOW FAR AWAY IS THE PARKING FROM THE UNIT?

A  Find this out! It's a definite issue when the weather is bad!


## MAINTENANCE

Q  HOW DO I KNOW WHICH PARTS OF MY UNIT THAT
I MUST MAINTAIN?

A  The *Declaration* will state items that are the owner's
responsibility to maintain and/or replace. This issue is
<u>very</u> important to know before you buy. In some
condominium associations, owners are even responsible
for maintaining and replacing the <u>exteriors</u> of their units,
such as siding and roofs. This may cause a major
financial issue for the owner, so prospective buyers <u>must</u>
know whether this or other similar requirements exist.

Q  WHAT ABOUT TRASH DISPOSAL?

A  All condominium associations have rules regarding trash
disposal and you will need to find out what they are.
Some associations contract with the hauler, but owners
must provide their own containers. Some associations
have dumpsters and some have individual pickup. There
are usually restrictions on when and where individual
containers can be placed, both for pickup and storage.
Some associations require containers to be stored in
garages or out of sight.

Q  WILL I BE ABLE TO MAKE CHANGES IN MY CONDO
IF I DON'T LIKE SOMETHING?

A  The definition of common and limited common elements
in the *Declaration* will help you determine whether you

may alter a portion of your living space. Clearly, you will not have the authority to make any change that may affect the structural integrity of the building without permission from the Board of Directors.

Q DO I HAVE TO CUT THE GRASS OR REMOVE SNOW?

A The *Declaration* may state who is responsible for these items. Check the "Management Maintenance, Repairs, and Replacement of Common Elements and Facilities" section. If not covered, the association may have adopted rules addressing these issues. In any case, the association will normally contract for these services. The key is to know which areas the association's contractors will maintain and which areas are your responsibility.

Q HOW QUICKLY ARE REPAIRS MADE?

A The process of getting repairs completed is different than when you were the only one making the decision. If a common element needs repair/replacement, you will notify the association, through the management company. If the management company has authority for that repair, it should be completed in a timely fashion. However, if the repair is outside the management company's scope of authority, they must present the issue to the board for approval.

## LIFESTYLE

Q IF THERE ARE RECREATIONAL FACILITIES, IS THEIR USE INCLUDED IN THE CONDOMINIUM FEE?

A There may be an extra fee for rental or use of a recreational facility, chargeable to unit owners. The

*Declaration* and/or rules will state whether the
association can charge extra for the use of the
association's recreational facilities. Some associations
retain an outside source to run an exercise room, pool,
party area, golf course, etc. Some facilities are internally
operated. The association usually subsidizes the
recreational facilities to some degree, either through the
regular assessments or usage fees to owners.

Q  IS THE LIFESTYLE OR AMBIENCE SATISFACTORY
TO ME?

A  Some buildings have age restrictions. Some
associations allow pets and others ban them. Some
complexes have a high tenant-to-owner ratio. Many
factors affect the pride of ownership and community.
Finding answers to these kinds of questions will tell
you whether the unit and association are compatible
with your requirements.

Q  ARE THERE PLANNED SOCIAL EVENTS?

A  Many associations plan various types of social events.
The recreational facilities will naturally create some.
Events may be planned by the board, committees, or
individual owners. The answer to this question may have
a bearing on the "lifestyle" of the community.

Q  ARE THERE ANY PLANS TO CHANGE THE
RECREATIONAL FACILITIES?

A  A change in the recreational facilities may affect the
property value of your unit and your assessment
(maintenance fees). The Board of Directors and/or the
management company should be able to tell you.

Q   DOES THE ASSOCIATION REGULARLY PRODUCE A
    NEWSLETTER?

A   Newsletters are one of the most effective means of
    communication between the Board of Directors and
    the owners. If there is no newsletter, the owners may
    find it difficult to know what is happening in the
    community.

## MONEY

Q   DO I HAVE TO PAY THE UTILITIES?

A   Yes, in one of several ways. The *Declaration* addresses
    this issue. Normally, each unit is responsible for directly
    paying the utilities that are individually metered.
    Depending on the design of the buildings, some utilities
    may be billed from a master meter. In those cases, the
    association will either pay out of the assessments
    (maintenance fees) or bill the unit's share back to the
    owner. Therefore, you will either be personally invoiced
    by the utility companies, pay the bill by way of your
    assessments (maintenance fees), or be billed back by the
    association.

Q   DO I HAVE TO PAY ANY FEES TO THE ASSOCIA-
    TION IF I RENT OR SELL MY UNIT?

A   This issue may be addressed in the *Declaration*, but
    usually the rules will specify. There may be a leasing fee
    required by the association. There will usually be an
    escrow fee when a unit is sold, payable to either the
    association or the managing agent.

Q  ARE THERE TAX ADVANTAGES TO OWNING
    A CONDO?

A  If your unit is mortgaged, you may be able to deduct the
    interest. Check with your accountant.

Q  WAS A RESERVE STUDY DONE AND WHEN?

A  If a study has been done recently, it will give you
    confidence that the board knows the future financial
    requirements for replacing the major components of the
    property. This will minimize the need for special
    assessments.

Q  IS THERE A SPECIAL ASSESSMENT CURRENTLY
    OR IS ONE PLANNED?

A  A special assessment may be in place due to an emergency
    situation or a lack of reserve funds due to poor planning.
    The Board of Directors decides whether one is necessary.
    The association's financial documents should give you
    important information. The health of the reserve fund
    will have a definite impact on your future financial
    obligations.

Q  CAN I PAY THE SPECIAL ASSESSMENT OVER
    TIME OR DOES IT HAVE TO BE PAID ALL
    AT ONCE?

A  When a special assessment is levied, the Board of
    Directors establishes the amount of the assessment and
    how the owners will be required to pay. If the amount of
    the assessment is very large, the board may offer the
    owners a payment plan. However, special assessments
    may be due immediately.

Q  WHAT CAUSES A SPECIAL ASSESSMENT?

A  The association is responsible for keeping the property in
   good condition, regardless of cost. Unlike living in a
   single dwelling, an expensive repair or replacement in a
   condominium development cannot be postponed because
   of a cash shortage. Depending on the financial health of
   the association, reserve funds should be used for the
   expensive items that are not included in the operating
   budget. If the reserve funds are inadequate, the unit
   owners may be specially assessed.

Q  HOW ARE ASSESSMENTS (MAINTENANCE FEES)
   DETERMINED?

A  The Board of Directors creates the operating budget,
   usually every fiscal year. Included in that budget are
   the expenses for all services provided to the
   association, plus an amount to be put into the reserve
   (replacement) fund. That total budget is then divided
   among all owners according to their individual
   percentage of ownership interest in the association.
   Each unit's percentage of ownership is established by
   the *Declaration*.

Q  HOW OFTEN WILL THE CONDOMINIUM ASSESS-
   MENTS CHANGE?

A  Historically, the assessments (maintenance fees) increase
   on a fairly regular basis. The Board of Directors creates
   the budget each fiscal year. The budget determines the
   amount of each owner's assessment (maintenance fee).
   Fees fluctuate depending on changing expenses, just
   as your expenses would change if you were in a single-
   family home.

**Q WILL MY UNIT APPRECIATE IN VALUE? IS IT A GOOD INVESTMENT?**

A    Several factors affect the answer to this question. Some of this information can be gathered online. Other sources are the local Chamber of Commerce, government administrative offices, and the board of education.

- Is the association well managed?
- Is it close to good schools?
- It is in a low-crime area?
- Does it have a particular "draw," such as a beach/lake, progressive downtown district, or desirable suburban location?
- Does the residential setting have a good mix of single-family homes and apartments? If there are too many apartments, the population density will be high, which may deter future buyers.
- Is there easy access to freeways, mass transit, and airports?
- Are shopping and recreation close by?
- Does it have good "curb appeal"?
- Is the unit you are considering located in the most appealing area within the complex?
- Is the property located on a busy street(s)?
- Is the unit near garages or carports where cars are constantly coming and going?
- Are the units spread far apart, allowing for some degree of privacy?
- Do you have to walk around several other units to get to your unit?
- Is the entrance to the unit individual or a common entrance used by several units?
- Is there ample lighting from windows, doors, skylights?

- Does the unit have modern appliances and decorating?
- Is the unit large enough for you to enjoy and still command a reasonable price for a quick resale later?
- Does the interior layout seem logical or awkward?

## BUSINESS

Q HOW IS THE PROPERTY BEING MANAGED?

A The majority of associations are managed by professional management companies, which is definitely a plus. However, some are self-managed. If managed by the owners, the association may expect a high level of volunteer work. The expertise and competence of the members of the Board of Directors will have an impact on how well the association will be operated.

Q WHEN WAS THE LAST TIME THE BOARD DID AN OWNER SURVEY AND WHY?

A This is an important question because it will give you some idea of whether the board seeks owner input before making decisions. Minutes of the annual meetings, committee meetings, and board meetings should give you this information. The association's newsletter is also an excellent source.

Q DOES THE ASSOCIATION HAVE EMPLOYEES?

A Whether the association employs its own workers or hires outside contractors may have some bearing on the quality and timeliness of services. This issue may also affect the budget and, therefore, the owners' fees. The Board of Directors, the management company, and the residents will be able to give you this information.

## LEGAL

Q  WHAT ARE *AMENDMENTS?*

A  Both the *Declaration* and *Bylaws* may be amended by the
association. *Amendments* address issues in the *Declaration*
and *Bylaws* that are either missing or need changed.
Amending the governing documents usually requires an
ownership vote. The percentage of the vote to pass is stated
in the *Declaration.* Any item in the governing documents
may be changed by *Amendments*, so it is very important to
know which, if any, have already been changed.

Q  IF I DECIDE TO SELL, DOES THE ASSOCIATION
HAVE THE FIRST OPTION TO BUY?

A  Normally, this answer is found in the *Declaration.* If the
*Declaration* is silent on the subject and there is no
*Amendment*, the association will not have the first option
to buy. The legal term for this is "first right of refusal."

Q  DOES THE ASSOCIATION NEED AN ATTORNEY?

A  An attorney is <u>very</u> important to an association. Usually,
the attorney will handle the collection of delinquent
accounts and represent the association if there are any
lawsuits. However, an attorney who is hired by the
association is completely committed to it. He/she cannot
represent individual owners.

Q  ARE THERE CURRENTLY ANY LAWSUITS OR
LEGAL PROCEEDINGS?

A  If there are, there may be unexpected legal expenses that
will ultimately come out of the unit owners' pockets.
There will be no way to predict whether the association

will prevail: therefore, there is no way to know if funding will be forthcoming or will have to be paid by the owners.

## COMPLAINTS

Q WHAT IF I DON'T LIKE THE WAY THE ASSOCIATION IS BEING RUN?

A You have different ways in which to express your concerns. You may become a member of the Board of Directors or an ad hoc committee, or ask to be heard at an annual or a board meeting. In any case, you should present your request in writing, in advance of a regular board meeting. <u>Under no condition should you withhold payment of your maintenance fees or place your fees in escrow.</u> If you withhold assessments, the board will probably initiate a collection action against you.

Q WHAT IF MY NEIGHBOR BOTHERS ME WITH LOUD MUSIC OR LATE NIGHT PARTIES?

A Most associations have a procedure for filing complaints. Usually, the complaint must be presented in writing to either the Board of Directors or the managing agent. Normally, the alleged violator will be contacted and a reasonable effort will be made to gain the violator's agreement to cease the violation. There should be penalty provisions in the governing documents or rules if the efforts to gain compliance are unsuccessful.

Q HOW SOUNDPROOF IS THE STRUCTURE?

A The building(s) will be more soundproof if the floors and walls are concrete. Wood frame construction will transmit noise much more than concrete. The Declaration should list the construction materials, or the association's insurance agent may be able to provide this information.

Q  DOES MY OPINION COUNT?

A  Absolutely! You will become part of a community when you purchase a unit. You will vote on issues according to your percentage of ownership of the corporation. You may have more input if you become a board member or join a committee.

> *There are checklists in the chapter titled "Kay's Exclusive Condo Buyer's Checklists" that you can use as you investigate various condominium complexes. Checklists are also available to <u>download</u> in 8.5 × 11 inch format from our website at:* **www.condo-condominium.com**

 *WHAT'S NEXT? Now you need to know where to find the answers to these questions for your specific unit.*

# WHAT LAWS GOVERN A CONDOMINIUM?

> *Why be bothered with all these "governing documents"?*
> *Can't I just move in and worry about them later?*
> *If I do want them, where do I get copies?*

The San Francisco-based Citizens Against Private Government talks about the fact that buyers typically don't get a copy of an association's governing documents until they close on their home or move in. At that point, it's usually too late to back out. Also, the governing documents often are written in legalese, so a buyer may not understand the Rules or the consequences of not abiding by them.

Q  WHAT GOVERNMENT LAWS APPLY TO CONDO-MINIUM ASSOCIATIONS?

A  They are as follows:

1. <u>The United States Constitution</u> states that persons cannot be deprived of their property without due process. For condominium owners, due process mandates that an owner has the right to a hearing before any penalty may be assessed.

2. <u>Federal law</u> requires all associations to file a tax return every year. In addition, it prohibits discrimination against children, the handicapped, etc.

3. <u>Every state</u> has a State Condominium Act that provides for the establishment of condominiums as legal entities. In general, state statutes permit condominiums to incorporate as either regular or not-for-profit corporations. However, incorporation may or may not be a legal requirement.

4. <u>Municipal laws</u> only apply in the particular municipality in which the association is located. For example, some local governments have ordinances that prohibit barbecue grilling on balconies and many have pet ordinances.

### Q WHY DO ASSOCIATIONS HAVE GOVERNING DOCUMENTS?

A The purpose of an association's governing documents is to provide for the legal structure and operation of the community. These documents:

☺ Define the rights and obligations of both the association and its owners:
  • Create a legal, binding relationship between the association and each owner
  • Establish the mechanisms for governing and funding the association's operations
☺ Set forth rules and standards for the:
  • Protection of both the owners and the community
  • Enhancement of property values
  • Promotion of harmonious living

### Q WHAT ARE THE SPECIFIC DOCUMENTS THAT GOVERN EACH CONDOMINIUM ASSOCIATION?

A *Recorded Map, Plat or Plan, Articles of Incorporation* (if incorporated), *Declaration of Condominium*

*Ownership, Amendments, Master Deed, Bylaws* and Rules (sometimes called regulations or resolutions).

 *Buyer's Tip—As a buyer, you can get the Declaration, Amendments, Bylaws and Rules from the seller, the realtor, the Board of Directors, the management company, or from local government offices. As an owner, you can get copies from the Board of Directors, the management company, or government offices. The Recorded Map, Plat or Plan and Master Deed are filed at the local government office. The Articles of Incorporation are filed with the state and should be available on the Internet.*

## Q  WHO CREATES OR WRITES THE GOVERNING DOCUMENTS?

A  The declarant (developer) creates and files the *Plat, Map or Plan, Articles of Incorporation* (if incorporated), the *Master Deed, Declaration* and *Bylaws. Amendments* are created by the Board of Directors and approved by the owners. The association's Board of Directors creates Rules or Resolutions.

## Q  WHAT IS THE PURPOSE OF EACH DOCUMENT?

A  The *Plat, Map* or *Plan:*

1. Shows the precise location of each unit, as well as the common elements and facilities of the association
2. Defines an owner's or a community's title to property
3. Helps to determine who is responsible for maintaining a particular piece of property

4. Determines whether a property improvement is properly located

5. Must be recorded in the local land records office before any units shown on it are sold

A   The *Articles of Incorporation* (if incorporated):

1. Bring the corporation into existence and provide a corporate wall of protection for the association

2. Define the corporation's basic purposes and powers

3. Indicate whether stock will be issued

4. Indicate whether there will be a Board of Directors and, if so, identify the initial board

5. Must be filed with the appropriate state corporation agency

 *Buyer's Tip—Incorporation is very important for every association. The biggest benefit of incorporation is that it limits the liability of individual owners for what the community association does. **Limiting liability reduces financial exposure!***

A   The *Master Deed:*

1. Contains the "bundle" of rights or "chain of title" for ownership of the land

2. Must be recorded in the local land records office

A   The *Declaration:*

1. Defines the bundle of rights for each piece of real estate in the association

2. States the terms that are binding on the real estate itself, as well as on its original and succeeding purchasers

3. Brings the condominium into existence when it is filed in the office of the local recorder of deeds or registrar of titles

4. Defines the portions of the development owned by the owners and those owned by the community association

5. Creates relationships binding on all owners to one another and the association for the purposes of funding, governing, and maintaining the development

6. Establishes protective standards, restrictions, and obligations in areas ranging from architectural control to prohibitions on various activities in order to promote harmonious living

7. Creates the general administrative framework for the operation and management of the community association

8. Provides for transition of control from the declarant (developer) to the owners

9. May be amended by the affirmative vote of a percentage of owners (the percentage is stated in each *Declaration*)

10. Must be recorded in the local land records office—amendments must also be recorded

A   The *Bylaws:*

1. Govern the administration and management of the association

2. Can be part of the *Declaration* or adopted as soon as a corporation is established

3. State the requirements for membership in the association

4. State the requirements for membership meetings

5. Set the voting rights of member owners

6. Contain the procedures for electing the Board of Directors and officers

7. Enumerate the general powers and duties of the board

8. Provide for indemnification of officers and directors (except in cases of gross negligence or willful misconduct)

9. May be amended by the affirmative vote of a percentage of owners (the percentage is stated in each *Declaration* and/or *Bylaws*)

10. Must be recorded in the local land records office—amendments must also be recorded

A    The Rules or Resolutions:

1. Are created and formally adopted by the Board of Directors

2. Maintain, preserve, enhance, and protect the property values and assets of the association

3. Promote conformity and harmonious community living

4. Protect the freedom and safety of community residents

5. Affect owners' rights and obligations

6. Create a sense of fairness and equity among residents

7. Identify the expected behavior of residents and guests

8. Address the internal operations of the community association

9. Apply policies or rules to an individual situation

10. Describe routine events such as the adoption of a budget or approval of a contract

11. Must be properly published to all owners and occupants

12. Must not conflict with federal, state, and local laws and ordinances

13. Must not conflict with the association's *Declaration* and *Bylaws*

All of the governing documents are easily accessed.

**That's why most Boards of Directors have very little patience with owners who break the rules!**

*WHAT'S NEXT? The Declaration of Condominium Ownership—in plain English!*

# THE DECLARATION OF CONDOMINIUM OWNERSHIP

Discover the important answers to questions like these:

- *May I have a pet?*
- *Where do I park?*
- *What do I have to pay for?*
- *May I lease my unit?*
- *May I run a business in my unit?*
- *May I add a deck or patio?*

An owner in Florida spent $3,500 to have a landscaper install plants, planters, and sprinklers in his front yard. However, the association's Declaration didn't allow installing anything in front yards between the unit and the sidewalk. The owner and the association tried to work out a compromise rather than forcing the owner to dig up all the additions. If no compromise had been reached by the deadline for compliance, the owner could have been required to appear before a committee, which could have fined him $100 a day until the problem was corrected. The owner and the association did reach a compromise; the association agreed to allow all the plants and the sprinkler system to remain, and the owner agreed to remove the planters.

This chapter will reveal the Articles or Sections of the *Declaration of Condominium Ownership* that will have the most significant effect on your buying decision. **Take special note of those Articles followed by the Buyer's Tips.**

1. <u>Legal Descriptions and Definitions</u>—This Article contains the boundaries of the entire condominium association property and the meanings of some of the terminology used in the *Declaration*. It also states the government records office where the *Declaration* is filed and shows the volume and page numbers so that it can be easily located.

 *Buyer's Tip—Any unfamiliar terms in this chapter can be found in the Glossary.*

2. <u>Establishment of Condominium and Division of Condominium Property</u>—This Article states who is the owner/declarant (developer) of the property and the State Law/Code under which the community association is governed.

3. <u>Name</u>—The legal name of the property.

4. <u>Description of Property and Units</u>—This Article contains the general description of the property, construction materials, number of buildings, number of rooms and floors, and boundaries of the units. Each owner also has the ownership of an undivided interest of the common elements and facilities in the percentages <u>determined by the declarant (developer)</u> and expressed later in the *Declaration*.

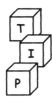

*Buyer's Tip—This section states how many units are built under this phase if this is a "phased" condominium. If this condominium is __not__ phased, the Declaration will state the total number of units. The numbers of units being built in future phases are covered by Declaration Amendments. **The total number of units __directly__ affects the amount of the assessments (maintenance fees).***

5. <u>Common Elements (also called Common Areas) and Facilities</u>—This Article contains the description and ownership of the common elements and facilities, <u>excluding the units</u>. Examples of common elements and facilities are roofs, lawns, and swimming pool. Percentages of ownership (also called percentages of interest), by unit, are listed here if they do not have a section of their own later in the *Declaration*.

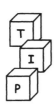

*Buyer's Tip—Owners' assessments (maintenance fees) will be higher in communities with recreational facilities.*

6. <u>Limited Common Elements (also called Limited Common Areas) and Facilities</u>—This Article states that each unit owner has exclusive and irrevocable license to use and occupy the limited common elements and facilities and defines what those areas are. Examples of limited common elements and facilities are balconies, patios, and pads for placement of central air conditioning compressors.

7. <u>Easements</u>—This Article grants rights of access and use for different parts of the property and units to the

declarant (developer), managing agent, owners, and residents of units.

8. <u>Association</u>—This Article establishes the legal name of the association and who is included in membership. It also states whether the association is a non-profit corporation, how it is to be governed, and the initial members of the Board of Directors.

9. <u>Agent for Service of Process</u>—This Article states the name and address of the initial person who is the Statutory Agent of the corporation (association) and the method by which the Agent may be changed.

10. <u>Management, Maintenance, Repairs, and Replacement of Common Elements (also called Common Areas) and Facilities</u>—This Article states warranties furnished by the declarant (developer). It defines differences between the association's and the unit owners' responsibilities for providing maintenance, repairs, and replacement of the common elements and the limited common elements. NOTE—this is <u>NOT</u> to be confused with ownership and use as explained in 5 and 6 above.

 *Buyer's Tip—This section states what parts of your unit you must maintain and/or replace at <u>your own expense</u>. It also states what part of the property is the association's obligation.*

11. <u>Common Expenses and Assessments</u>—This Article states that the profits and expenses of the association shall be distributed to and assessed against the unit owners according to the percentages of ownership (also called percentages of interest) of their respective units in the common elements and facilities. It also explains the

method of payments, the date(s) payments are due, and the penalties for non-payments and late payments. These penalties may include, but are not limited to, late fees, loss of privileges of use of the common elements and facilities, and the method by which liens and foreclosure may be filed by the association against a unit.

*Buyer's Tip—Find out if the owners' assessments (maintenance fees) are due in one lump sum at the beginning of the fiscal year, or if they may be paid on a monthly basis throughout the year. Also, find out if there is a grace period before penalties are added.*

12. <u>Restrictions as to Use and Occupancy of Condominium Property</u>—This Article describes restrictions for the common elements, facilities, and units.

*Buyer's Tip—This is where you will find whether you can lease your unit or have a pet; it also covers what kind of vehicles and activities are prohibited. These are just a few examples; there may be more!*

13. <u>Insurance</u>—Every association needs at least four types of insurance: a) Property, b) Directors & Officers Liability, c) General Liability, and d) Casualty. This Article also defines the authority to purchase insurance and the minimal amounts of coverage for each type.

14. <u>Reconstruction or Repair of Damage</u>—This Article details the association's and unit owners' responsibilities for reconstruction or repair after a casualty.

15. <u>Rehabilitation of Existing Building</u>—This Article states the requirement for determining if the property is partly

or completely obsolete and whether to have it renewed and rehabilitated.

16. <u>Additions to the Condominium Property</u>—This Article gives declarant (developer) the right and option to expand the condominium from time to time in one or more phases by constructing residential buildings and other improvements and utilities to service them. The Article also states the period of time the declarant (developer) has to do this.

17. <u>Amendment of Declaration</u>—This Article describes the procedure and percentage of ownership required to change any Article of the *Declaration*, abandon the condominium regime, change the percentage of ownership, and subdivide any unit or the common elements. NOTE—changes in the *Declaration* may affect assessments for the common elements and facilities, depending on the nature of the amendment.

18. <u>Removal of Property from Provisions of the State Law Governing Condominiums</u>—This Article describes the procedure and percentage of ownership required to remove the condominium property from the provisions of the state law governing condominiums.

19. <u>Remedies for Breach of Covenants and Rules</u>—This Article states the association's rights to remedy any violation or breach of covenant/provision of the *Declaration*, *Bylaws*, or rules.

20. <u>Sale of Ownership Property</u>—This Article states whether the association has the first right of refusal or whether the association has the first option to buy before the seller can list the unit with a realtor or personally sell it. This Article provides the procedure the association and the seller must follow if the association purchases or declines to purchase the unit.

21. <u>Condemnation</u>—If the property is condemned and either partially or entirely taken by the condemning authorities, this Article outlines the procedure for doing so.

22. <u>Miscellaneous Provisions</u>—Included here are topics that were not included in the other Articles, such as, but not limited to, declarant's (developer's) rights pending sale of units, notices of mortgagees, books and records, termination, waiver, severability, interpretation, and gender references.

---

The *Declaration of Condominium Ownership* contains important information such as:

- *What you own*
- *What you can change*
- *What you are responsible to maintain*
- *How you pay assessments*
- *Penalties for late payments or for non-payment*
- *Restrictions for use and occupancy*
- *Insurance requirements*
- *How the Declaration can be changed*

This, along with the *Bylaws*, is the ***most important*** information you need to know before you purchase.

---

*WHAT'S NEXT? The Bylaws—**in plain English!***

# THE BYLAWS

Discover the important answers to questions like these:

- *Who belongs to the association?*
- *What are my voting rights?*
- *What issues can I vote on?*
- *What powers belong to the Board of Directors?*
- *How are board members elected?*
- *How often are the meetings held?*
- *Who prepares the budget?*

How does the typical buyer and owner go about requesting and accessing the books and records of the condominium association? According to the Bylaws, associations must maintain copies of all governing documents, amendments to those documents, and the rules to ensure the availability of those documents to prospective buyers and unit owners.

Understanding the *Bylaws* will save money and reduce frustration because you will know how the association is supposed to operate. Pay special attention to the Articles on the Board of Directors, General Powers of the Association, and Finances of the Association.

1. <u>Definitions</u>—This Article contains the meanings of some of the terminology used in the *Bylaws*.

*Buyer's Tip—Any unfamiliar terms in this chapter can be found in the Glossary.*

2. <u>Unit Owners' Association</u>
   a. *Name*—Legal name of the association.
   b. *Membership*—All unit owners are members.
   c. *Voting Rights*—Members are entitled to vote according to their ownership percentage.
   d. *Proxies*—Voting may or may not be permitted by proxy.
   e. *Meetings of Members*—Annual and Special.
   f. *Notice of Meetings*—Sent by the association secretary.
   g. *Quorum*—Requirements for an official meeting.
   h. *Order of Business*—Agenda for the Annual Meeting.
   i. *Conduct of Meetings*—Robert's Rules of Order.

*Buyer's Tip—Take note of who belongs to the association and what the voting rights are. Types and number of meetings for <u>owners</u> will also be stated here.*

3. <u>Board of Directors</u>
   a. *Number and Qualifications*—How many members and their requirements.
   b. *Nomination*—May be by a committee and/or from the floor.
   c. *Vacancies*—How to fill board vacancies.

d. *Organizational Meeting*—For the board to elect its officers.
e. *Regular Meetings*—The number required.
f. *Special Meetings*—What the requirements are to call one.
g. *Executive Session*—The reason(s) why they are closed to association members.
h. *Quorum*—Requirements for an official meeting.
i. *Compensation*—Board members are not permitted to be compensated.
j. *Fidelity Bonds*—Requirements for bonding of board members.
k. *Powers and Duties*
   1. Adopt and publish rules.
   2. Declare the office of a member of the board to be vacant.
   3. Employ a manager, an independent contractor, or other employees.
   4. Prepare and adopt an annual budget.
   5. Establish the methods of collecting assessments.
   6. Collect unit owner assessments and make deposits into association's accounts.
   7. Provide for the operation and maintenance of the common property.
   8. Pay for the cost of services out of the common assessments.
   9. Contract for repairs, additions, and improvements after a catastrophe.
   10. Obtain, carry, and pay premiums for insurance on the common elements and facilities.
   11. Enforce the provisions of the *Declaration*, *Bylaws*, and rules.

12. Notify unit owners of any litigation against the association.

13. Keep books with detailed accounts of receipts and expenditures.

14. Borrow money for the operation, upkeep, care, and maintenance of the common elements and facilities.

15. Delegate duties and responsibilities to persons, firms, corporations, or a managing agent.

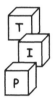

*Buyer's Tip—Under "Qualifications," you will find out if non-owners can be elected to the Board of Directors—you want to know who is in control of your money! Types and number of <u>board</u> meetings will be stated here. Powers and Duties of the Board of Directors are <u>extremely</u> important because they directly affect the owners' assessments (maintenance fees).*

4. <u>Officers and Their Duties</u>—The principal officers of the association are the president, vice president, secretary, and treasurer, all of whom are elected by the Board of Directors at the organizational meeting following each annual meeting of the association. The same person may not hold the offices of president and treasurer simultaneously. Duties of the officers are as follows:

a. *President*—The president is the chief executive officer of the association and presides at all meetings of the association and the board. The president makes sure that orders of the board are carried out and signs all legal documents and contracts on behalf of the association.

b. *Vice President*—The vice president takes the place of the president and performs the duties of the president in his absence or inability to act.

c. *Secretary*—The secretary records votes, keeps the minutes of all meetings, sends out meeting notices, and keeps the owner roster up to date.

d. *Treasurer*—The treasurer is responsible for the association's funds and securities, keeps full and accurate financial records of account showing receipts and disbursements, deposits all monies in the association's accounts, and signs all checks and promissory notes.

5. Committees—Committees are appointed by the board for specific tasks and lengths of time. Committees have no authority to implement any solutions or functions but must advise the board of their findings and conclusions on all matters assigned to them.

6. General Powers of the Association—The association pays all expenses for the common condominium property, such as the following:

a. *Casualty Insurance*—Casualty insurance insuring the common elements and facilities.

b. *Liability Insurance*—Liability insurance insuring the unit owners and occupants against liability for personal injury, disease, illness or death, or for injury to or destruction of property arising from the common elements and facilities.

c. *Directors & Officers Liability Insurance*—The board should be insured by the association against dishonesty, slander, libel, and gross negligence.

d. *Workers' Compensation Insurance*

e. *Wages and Fees for Services*—The wages and fees for management, maintenance, legal counsel, accounting services, and rule enforcement.

f. *Care of the Common Elements and Facilities*—The cost of landscaping, gardening, snow removal, painting, cleaning, maintaining, decorating, repairing, and replacing of the common elements and facilities, <u>excluding</u> the limited common elements and facilities.

g. *Additional Expenses*—The cost of all materials, labor, services, and replacements necessary to maintain the common condominium property.

h. *Association's Right to Enter Units*—The Association or its agents may enter any unit to repair or construct an item that is the association's responsibility. In the event of an emergency, any person or entity authorized by the board may immediately access the unit, whether or not the unit owner is present.

i. *Capital Additions and Improvements*—When the board determines a portion of the common elements and facilities requires an addition, alteration, or improvement (as opposed to maintenance, repair, and replacement), they will proceed and the cost becomes a common expense.

 *Buyer's Tip—Under "i" above, find out what the maximum amount of money is that the Board of Directors can spend for a capital item. Then you will know at what level the board is required to obtain a vote of the owners. Many times, this issue will cause a special assessment!*

7. <u>Finances of the Association</u>

a. *Preparation and Approval of Budget*—According to the timeframe specified, the Board of Directors will adopt a budget for the amount necessary to pay all the common expenses for the next fiscal year, including an amount for replacement reserves, and send each unit owner a copy.

b. *Failure to Prepare Annual Budget*—The failure or delay of the board to prepare or deliver the annual budget to a unit owner does not release the owner from the obligation to pay his portion of the common assessment.

c. *Payment of Common Expenses*—Each unit owner must pay the common expenses assessed by the board.

d. *Annual Audit*—The books of the association should be audited once a year by an auditor who is not a member of the association.

 *Buyer's Tip—Note who prepares the budget and when owners must be notified of the budget for the new fiscal year. The annual budget <u>directly determines</u> each owner's assessment. It is <u>critical</u> that the financial records of the association be audited annually by a person who is <u>not</u> a member of the association in order to reduce the possibility of theft of the association's money!*

8. General Provisions

a. *Conflict of Interest*—This Article of the *Bylaws* states the conditions under which an actual or potential conflict of interest exists.

b. *Indemnification*—This section states the requirements for indemnification of a current or past board member.

c. *Amendments*—The *Bylaws* may be amended by the affirmative vote of the percentage of ownership stated in the *Declaration* and/or the *Bylaws*.

---

The *Bylaws* contain important information such as:

- *Association management*
- *Association membership*
- *Frequency of meetings*
- *Attendance at meetings*
- *Issues requiring owner vote*
- *Board member election procedures*
- *Budget preparation and notification*
- *Powers and duties of the board*

---

*WHAT'S NEXT? Along with the critical information in the Bylaws are the Rules. Rules are not to be confused with the Declaration and Bylaws, and they are discussed in the next chapter.*

# THE RULES

---

**Rules reveal critical details!**

The rules are for items that are unclear or not covered in the *Declaration, Bylaws* and *Amendments*. Sometimes, rules refine or give more detail to a restriction. Here are a couple of examples:

- *The Declaration may state you are permitted to have a dog. Rules could be made on issues such as whether a leash is required when the dog is outside, where it can be walked, and who is responsible for cleaning up soiling.*
- *The Declaration may permit you to lease your unit. The rules could state that the lease agreement must be subject to the governing documents and that the names of the residents must be given to the board.*

---

The Bylaws of a Florida condominium require basketball hoops to be put inside between dusk and dawn. Owners of a unit there say they have a tough time when it comes to dragging the hoop inside. They received a $500 fine, even after they appeared in front of board members to explain. They stated the association was making an example of them by selectively enforcing rules that were too strict. However, when they read through the Bylaws, they realized they were breaking some rules they didn't even know existed. One of them stated that residents were not even allowed to leave their garage doors open unless they were coming into or leaving their house. One of their neighbors told them that the rules are what they are, and the owners should have known it when they moved in.

Q  WHAT AREAS ARE NORMALLY COVERED
BY THE RULES?

A  Rules cover both the use of common elements and the individual units. They address the behavior of owners, tenants, and guests because of the possible impact of one person's behavior on another person.

"Conduct" rules frequently address the following issues:

- Pets
- Children
- Parking
- Solicitation
- Maintenance of units
- Leasing of units
- Use of common elements and facilities
- Garbage/trash
- Noise disturbances
- Outdoor equipment, such as play sets

"Architectural" rules frequently address the following issues:

- Fencing
- Decks and patios
- Exterior lighting
- Landscaping
- Doors

- Window treatments
- Roof protrusions, such as skylights

 *Buyer's Tip—Rule **violations** cause penalties! A conduct penalty may be an extra assessment that is added to your unit's account. An architectural penalty usually means the owner must remove and/or restore the item to its original standard—at his or her own expense!*

**Q WHO MAKES THE RULES?**

**A** The association makes them. This may happen through a committee formed by the Board of Directors or the board may create them. A committee does not have the authority to approve rules but gives its opinion to the board. Occasionally, the governing documents require the approval of some percentage of the owners before the rules take effect. State statutes and/or the *Declaration* and *Bylaws* give the association authority to enact rules it believes are necessary.

 *Buyer's Tip—An owner has no choice but to abide by the association's rules. Some owners decide to serve on a committee or the board in order to change rules they don't like.*

**Q HOW ARE THE RULES ENFORCED?**

**A** <u>Due Process</u>:

- All violations are handled in the same manner, as described in the rules.

- Use of due process is recognized by the courts as a legally valid enforcement.
- Most rule violations can be resolved by due process rather than going to court.
- The opportunity to be heard in a non-threatening forum is often enough to result in a person voluntarily obeying a rule.
- This process lends itself to exploring alternative means of resolution.

A   <u>Alternative Dispute Resolution (ADR)</u>:

- The association might propose ADR if confronted with a difficult rule violation or the possibility of litigation exists.
- The dispute is submitted to a trained, uninvolved third party for resolution.
- A rule violator might consider ADR if the person is dissatisfied with the association's decision.

A   <u>Internal Resources</u>:

- If an owner is found to be in violation of a rule, the board may impose penalties against the owner.
- Suspension of owner's voting rights
- Suspension of the use of common elements and recreational facilities
- Fines
- Eviction

A   <u>External Resources</u>:

Occasionally, the board may decide that an owner's violation can be better addressed by local authorities:

- Local Health Department
- Local Zoning Department

- Local Police
- Local Fire Department
- Local Building/Housing/Property Standards Department
- Local Animal Shelter or Animal Control Officer

Q EVERY CONDOMINIUM SHOULD HAVE A HAND-BOOK OF THE RULES.

A A Handbook should take all the legalese of the *Declaration, Bylaws,* and *Amendments* and boil them down into an easy-to-understand booklet. Also, there may be additional rules the association has created that could be included in the Handbook. It is much easier to read a condensed handbook than all of the governing documents. It is also much easier to find the Handbook than hunting through individual pieces of paper, each one containing one rule or resolution.

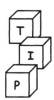

*Buyer's Tip—If your association does not have a Handbook, suggest the board prepare one, have one prepared, or form a committee to propose a draft.*

Q WHERE CAN I FIND THE RULES AND REGULATIONS?

1. In the *Declaration of Condominium Ownership* under "Restrictions"
2. In the *Bylaws*
3. In the *Amendments*
4. Handbook of Rules
5. The board should have a list of all the rules and resolutions.

**Q   DO THE RULES HAVE THE SAME AUTHORITY AS THE GOVERNING DOCUMENTS?**

A   Yes, because the association's governing documents enable them to be created as long as they do not contradict the governing documents. Note that rules do not need to be filed with any government agency.

---

The rules serve several purposes:

- *Rules promote harmonious community living.*
- *They maintain, preserve, enhance, and protect the property values and assets of the community.*
- *They satisfy the need to create a sense of fairness and equity among all residents.*
- *They should be consistently enforced.*

---

*WHAT'S NEXT? Now that you have a handle on the governing documents, let's talk about the financial issues.*

# LET'S TALK MONEY!

Avoid surprises!

Community associations are businesses, and their financial health requires careful oversight and monitoring.

Condominium experts are afraid that owners who cannot afford the maintenance fee increases and special assessments may soon abandon their units. If that happens, the owners remaining in the association will have to make up the missing share of money to maintain, repair, and replace the common elements and facilities—roofs, roads, landscaping, pools, etc. If there is a shortage of money, the service providers for the property are unlikely to feel sorry for the association and reduce their prices. Many condominium owners are older people and a $2,000 special assessment is hard to pay when living on a fixed income.

The association's governing documents and some government entities place financial requirements on the association. By knowing in advance what expenses will occur and being prepared for them by being familiar with approximately how much they will cost, the association should be able to handle them without special assessments.

There are four (4) main financial areas about which buyers and owners alike should be concerned:

1. Operating budget
2. Replacement (reserves) fund
3. Investments
4. Financial monitoring

## OPERATING BUDGET

- The operating budget is a financial plan or estimate of the community's income and expenses for a specific period of time, usually one (1) fiscal year.

- It indicates which services will be performed on the property and, therefore, which ones will <u>not</u> be performed.

- Federal, state and local governments also have requirements that the community will have to spend money to meet, i.e., ADA, employment, insurance.

- The income portion of the budget will indicate the amount received from the regular assessments (maintenance fees), as well as revenue from any other sources for that fiscal year.

- The expense portion of the budget will specify what services and amenities will be paid from the regular assessments (maintenance fees) for that fiscal year.

- If the operating income is not adequate, services and amenities may be reduced.

*Buyer's Tip—Look carefully at the bottom line (net income or loss). If it is a loss, you will know that either the Board of Directors did not budget properly or an unexpected expense occurred. In any case, one of four things will happen: the board will need to <u>borrow</u> from the replacement fund, <u>reduce</u> services to the owners, <u>increase</u> the next year's budget, or <u>specially assess</u> the owners.*

## REPLACEMENT (RESERVE) FUND

- The fund consists of monies put aside, in reserve, for the replacement of the major components of the association's common elements and facilities.
- Replacement funds, for the most part, come from a percentage of the owners' assessment fees (maintenance fees).
- It is a timetable for accumulating and spending funds for major items.
- Proof of a replacement fund may be required by a mortgage institution before it will lend money for the purchase of a unit.
- Maintaining a replacement fund enhances the resale value for all of the units in the association.
- The age, life expectancy, condition, and design of the property will determine the reserves needed for replacement.
- Make sure a Reserve Study has been completed within the last three (3) years and that the association is fully funding as stipulated in the Reserve Study.
- If the replacement (reserve) fund is not adequate, special assessments may be required.

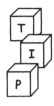

*Buyer's Tip—It is very easy to find out if the replacement fund is being fully funded. The association's annual operating budget should indicate the amount being set aside for this purpose. Compare that figure with the amount shown in the Reserve Study for that year—the two should match.*

## INVESTMENTS

- The association should have an overall investment strategy and both buyers and owners should find out what it is.
- Investment money should be held by insured institutions in low-risk instruments.
- The money should be liquid enough to be available when needed.
- The funds may not be safe if a qualified investment advisor has not been used.

## FINANCIAL MONITORING

- The Board of Directors should develop and enforce policies regarding investment policy, control of replacement funds (reserves), collections, maintenance of separate accounts for operating and replacement (reserve) monies, and checks and balances to ensure safety of funds.
- Monthly financial statements should be produced and available.
- All investments and accounts should be reconciled monthly or quarterly at a minimum.

- A financial analysis should be completed each year by an independent CPA in full cooperation with the Board of Directors, committees, and management.
- The insurance and bonding should be reviewed every year for adequacy.
- If these steps are not followed, the owners' monies may not be properly safeguarded.

 *Buyer's Tip—Make sure that the association's checking account, replacement (reserves) account, and investment accounts are NOT co-mingled with any other accounts. Each account should be in the name of the association and under the association's Federal identification number.*

## Q WHAT IF OWNERS DON'T PAY THEIR SHARE?

A An assessment (maintenance fee) is every owner's financial obligation to the community association and is a binding legal obligation based on the association's governing documents. As we have already discussed, owner assessments (maintenance fees) are the revenue source for the community.

If some owners do not pay, the bills must still be met. Even though delinquent owners may be in formal collection, the revenue stream is still reduced. In fact, there may be legal expenses for collection attorneys. Delinquent payments may have the following consequences:

- Assessments may have to be increased to cover the deficit.
- Some essential maintenance may become unaffordable.

- The property may begin to appear run-down which reduces property values.
- Shortfalls may need to be replaced by an increase in the next year's budget.
- Borrowing from otherwise restricted association funds may be necessary.
- Borrowing from a lending institution may be required.
- Disharmony between paying owners and delinquent ones may result.

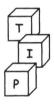 *Buyer's Tip—The association's financial balance sheet will show the accounts receivable amount, which is the amount owed by the owners but not yet paid to the association. When considering a loan application, lending institutions also look at the relationship between the accounts receivable amount and the amount set forth in the budget for owner assessments (maintenance fees).*

Q   WHO PREPARES THE BUDGETS?

A   Several different people may assist in budget preparation, but the Board of Directors has the ultimate responsibility for establishing, approving, and monitoring it. Many boards will delegate preparation to the managing agent and/or a finance committee. In any event, the board should invite owner input and review prior to approval.

Q   HOW DO I KNOW IF THE FINANCIAL PICTURE IS ADEQUATE?

A   The best way is to have financial statements and policies reviewed by an independent third party if you do not have financial expertise. An impartial third party, someone who is knowledgeable of community associations, can confirm you have selected a property that is financially healthy.

> One secret to saving money . . .
>
> It's been said that 97% of what occurs in any business or organization is predictable. The key is to be proactive about the 97%!

 *WHAT'S NEXT? You've been bombarded with tons of valuable information. Who can help you sort it all out?*

# WHO CAN HELP ME MAKE THE BEST DECISION?

How can you avoid moving into a condominium in which you may be unhappy?

*Do your homework before signing a contract.*

We, as Americans, all have the expectation that we will enjoy private property rights. This concept is at odds with community association rules. Rules are the best and worst aspects of community association living. Ideally, the rules enhance property values and promote community harmony. In reality, the rules may cause division in a community. Usually, it's not the rules themselves, but the board's inconsistent enforcement of them and making up new rules as they go that results in owners feeling their rights have been violated. Conflicts can arise between the board and the owners when the board ignores the rights of owners and arbitrarily enforces restrictions. <u>Be informed—find out as much as possible about the association before purchasing</u>. Speak with members of the board, with residents, the property manager, and any other persons with knowledge about the association. The financial, political, and legal conditions of your community association can affect your quality of life and the value of your unit.

People who can give you valuable information before you purchase:

- Real estate professionals
- The declarant (developer)
- The Board of Directors
- Residents
- The condominium management company
- A lending institution and title company
- An attorney
- The association's insurance agent
- The association's accountant

## REAL ESTATE PROFESSIONALS

Real estate professionals are one of the best sources of information in your decision-making process. ***But be aware that not all realtors are alike***. Having the right knowledge can literally make a difference of thousands of dollars out of your pocket over the life of your ownership.

- Look for real estate credentials. These are a sign the professional has earned and is maintaining a high level of expertise through continuing education.
- It is better to use someone who has been recommended by a satisfied customer. A word-of-mouth recommendation is more likely to lead to someone with integrity and who knows the value of personal service.
- Find someone who has expertise in the community association industry. Condominiums are **quite different**

from single-family homes and it is imperative that your agent know all the differences.

- They have access to a broad range of information, such as the Multiple Listing Service.
- They can provide "comparables" in the geographical area in which you are interested.

## THE DECLARANT (DEVELOPER)

If the community is still under construction, the declarant (developer) must give you a "Disclosure Package." It includes the *Declaration*, *Bylaws*, Architectural Committee Guidelines, Management Contract, Unit Descriptions, Layouts, Prices, and Warranties. It is important to remember that this package is usually written by an attorney. Therefore, you may need someone to interpret the *legalese* portions.

## THE BOARD OF DIRECTORS

The Board of Directors can provide all the legal documents used to govern the operation of the association. In addition, there will be other types of information that may give you the "feel" of the environment of the community. However, remember that the members of the board are volunteers. In addition, most of them probably work regular jobs. Their time may be limited.

*Buyer's Tip—One of the best ways to see the interactions between the owners and the board is to attend one of their meetings. You may request permission to attend personally or through your realtor.*

## RESIDENTS

One of the best ways to get the "flavor" of the community in which you are considering a purchase is to talk to those who live there. Feel free to knock on several doors, tell them you are a prospective buyer, and ask if they have time to answer some questions. *Regardless of what the governing documents say, you want to find out what living in this community is like directly from those who live there.*

## THE CONDOMINIUM MANAGEMENT COMPANY

It is usually better to live in a community that is professionally managed. There are some very well-run self-managed associations, but the board members are typically too busy to pay the proper amount of attention to association business. If there is a management company, the agents can be of great assistance when making a decision.

- Like people in real estate, professional management companies and agents receive credentials for learning information that's vital to the industry. They maintain their credentials with continuing education. However, there are a number of people who have gone into the management business without any education at all. Beware!
- Find out which duties the management company performs and which are performed by other outside contractors.
- It is important to find out if the management company has a good relationship with the Board of Directors. One indicator would be whether the management company attends all board meetings. Another sign would

be whether the management company or the board oversees employees and contractors working on the property.

- How the management company handles owner calls is vital. It is very important to know whether they have a live person on call 24/7, use an answering service, or rely on an answering machine. If you have an emergency in the middle of the night, you will want a quick response!

- Find out how often the property is inspected by the management company. Find out how often they do routine maintenance. Find out if the management company can make repairs as needed and/or when they need board approval.

- The management company will be able to inform you about the <u>age and condition</u> of the buildings and recreational facilities. This may give you some indication of the requirement for funding in the future.

- Is the management company bonded?

 *Buyer's Tip—Make an appointment with the association's property manager. This is probably the person with whom you will have the most contact after you move in. You can ask the manager all of the questions listed above.*

## LENDING INSTITUTION AND TITLE COMPANY

These two sources will help you decide HOW to buy and will ensure you receive a clear title. When comparing interest rates, remember that the true yield of the loan includes interest, points, and fees. Thus, it is possible for a low interest rate mortgage to cost more than one with a higher rate.

## Financing Sources Include:

- Banks
- Mortgage bankers
- Savings and loan institutions
- Online lenders
- Builders and developers
- Credit unions
- Mortgage brokers
- Sellers

 *Buyer's Tip—Your real estate agent should know the institutions with the lowest interest rates and the best title companies.*

## ATTORNEY, INSURANCE AGENT, AND ACCOUNTANT

All of these professionals are valuable in your decision-making process. Just as with the other professionals listed, they must meet specific standards to receive and maintain their licenses. It is important to find out their level of expertise with community associations.

### Attorney

If the association you are considering has an attorney, you will not be able to use him in any matter involving the association. However, you may be able to use him for a review of the association's documents. Of course, you may retain your own legal counsel for this purpose.

If you don't understand the governing documents of an association, you may be in for some surprises. These documents are often filled with so much legalese they require an attorney to decipher them. An attorney will be a valuable resource for explaining what the governing documents _really_ mean. The documents typically reviewed by an attorney are:

- *Declaration of Condominium Ownership*
- *Bylaws*
- *Articles of Incorporation*
- *Amendments*
- Rules, Regulations, Resolutions
- Management contract
- Collection Policy and Procedure

## The Association's Insurance Agent

The association's insurance agent plays a vital role in determining part of an owner's financial responsibility. There are two major concerns here—property and liability. Insurance can be tricky and you need to know how much insurance the association carries and what it covers in order to determine what you will need to cover. Your agent should review the following condominium association documents in order to determine the elements you need to insure:

- *Declaration of Condominium Ownership*
- *Bylaws*
- *Amendments* (any that pertain to insurance issues)
- Master insurance policy
- Risk management program

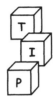

*Buyer's Tip—Because most of us are not insurance experts, it's a good idea to have the association's insurance agent talk to your insurance agent. Both of them will understand the insurance terminology in the governing documents and will be able to suggest the proper coverage for you.*

## The Association's Accountant

If the community association has an accountant, you most certainly should make an appointment to discuss the association's financial picture. Financial information is public knowledge. The accountant should be able to advise you on the following condominium association details:

- Current operating budget
- Year-end financial statements
- Long-range financial plan, including the Reserve Fund Study and plan
- Investments

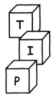

*Buyer's Tip—If possible, meet with the association's accountant. He or she can give you the answers you need regarding the budget, percentage of delinquent owners, and replacement (reserves) fund in a way you can understand quickly and easily.*

Take advantage of the expertise of qualified professionals so you can make the best possible decision about your new home and lifestyle.

**Look at the entire picture!**

*WHAT'S NEXT? Which documents do each of these professionals need to review?*

# 12
# WHAT DOCUMENTS SHOULD BE REVIEWED BEFORE YOU BUY?

*A comprehensive list of documents!*

- Administrative
- Financial
- Property

Pete thought he had done his homework before he bought his condo because he made sure he got copies of the Declaration and Bylaws. The day after he moved in, he noticed the neighbor's dog leaving a "present" on his front lawn. He reluctantly cleaned it up, hoping it was an isolated incident. As the days went by, he realized the neighbor's dog, as well as all the other pets living in the community, had the freedom to roam the entire property without being on leashes. He placed a call to the management company, only to find out there were absolutely NO pet rules! The problem, of course, was that Pete had received all the documents he needed, but he hadn't read them!

It is *vitally* important that buyers and owners completely understand all of these important documents and their requirements in order to live harmoniously in the community. Those who do not understand these documents may be "out of step" with those who do, potentially causing friction.

## ADMINISTRATIVE DOCUMENTS

- The Articles of Incorporation
- The Declaration of Condominium Ownership
- The Bylaws
- The association's rules
- Previous meeting minutes
- A list of committee types
- Newsletters
- The master insurance policy
- The Risk Management Program
- The Management Contract
- The Welcome Packet

## FINANCIAL DOCUMENTS

- The current Operating Budget
- The audited or reviewed year-end financial statements
- The Reserve Fund Study
- The Reserve Fund Plan
- The long-range financial plan
- List of investments
- The most current Balance Sheet and Profit/Loss statements
- Special Assessment information (past and proposed)
- The collection policy

## PHYSICAL PROPERTY DOCUMENTS

- Map indicating:
    1. The placement of units
    2. The location(s) of recreational facilities
    3. The location(s) of parking areas
    4. The location(s) of waste collection areas
    5. The location(s) of common elements
- A current site inspection report
- The preventive maintenance schedule
- The security system plan

> Even though the list of documents that should be reviewed is lengthy, taking the time for proper fact-finding will pay off.
>
> *The condominium in which you choose to live will be somewhat familiar to you even before you move in!*

 *WHAT'S NEXT? The next chapter will tell you what information you will find in each document.*

# THE LAST STEP
# BEFORE YOU BUY

We've already discussed why a review of the condominium documents is critical. Those documents are listed in the chapter titled "What Documents Should Be Reviewed Before You Buy?" This chapter lists the information you need to obtain from each document.

## THE ARTICLES OF INCORPORATION REVIEW

1. The date the association was incorporated
2. The legal name of the property
3. The definition of the purpose of the corporation
4. The identity of the initial Board of Directors

## THE DECLARATION OF CONDOMINIUM OWNERSHIP REVIEW

1. The date it was filed at the local land records office
2. The legal name of the association

3. The general description of property and construction
4. The list of recreational facilities
5. Those portions of the property owned by the association
6. Those portions of the property owned by the owners
7. The parts of the property that are the association's responsibility to maintain and/or replace
8. The parts of the property that are the owner's responsibility to maintain and/or replace
9. Restrictions and requirements for architecture, use and occupancy, and penalties for failure to comply for items such as:
   a. Pets
   b. Age restrictions
   c. Leasing of unit
   d. Parking
   e. Noise
   f. Business use
   g. Alteration of unit
   h. Enclosure of limited common elements
   i. Trash
   j. Storage
   k. Fences
   l. Decks/Patios
   m. Recreational equipment
   n. Landscaping
   o. Signs
   p. Prohibited activities
10. The association's insurance coverage requirements
11. The method for transition of control from the declarant (developer) to the owners (especially important to note if the complex is new)

12. The percentage of ownership for the unit being evaluated
13. The policies for payment of common assessments (maintenance fees) and collection
14. The percentage of unit owners required to amend the *Declaration* and *Bylaws*
15. Whether condominium expansion is permitted and the total number of units
16. The expansion timeframe
17. When control of the Board of Directors by the declarant (developer) will end

## THE BYLAWS REVIEW

1. The date they were filed at the local land records office
2. The requirements for association membership
3. The requirements for association and board meetings
4. The order of business at the annual meeting
5. Voting rights of unit owners
6. The procedure for electing the Board of Directors and officers
7. The number and qualifications for board members
8. The powers and duties of the board
9. The duties of each officer
10. The names of the mandatory committees
11. The procedure for preparation of the budget and notification to the unit owners

## THE AMENDMENTS TO THE DECLARATION AND BYLAWS REVIEW

1. The dates they were filed at the local land records office
2. The subject of each

# THE RULES, REGULATIONS AND/OR RESOLUTIONS REVIEW

1. Procedure for requesting permission from the Board of Directors for structural additions and/or changes
2. Prohibitions and requirements for decorations
3. Restrictions and procedures for use of the recreational facilities
4. Procedure for filing of complaints and complaint resolution
5. Location and restrictions of parking and vehicles
6. Pet restrictions
7. Location and rules for trash disposal
8. Procedure for leasing of units
9. Procedure for requesting permission from the Board of Directors to install a satellite dish
10. Noise restrictions
11. Rules for installation of signs
12. A list of prohibited activities


# THE MANAGEMENT COMPANY CONTRACT REVIEW

1. The name of the management company
2. Whether the contract is for full service or partial service
3. The length of time they have managed the association
4. Their professional credentials
5. The number of years they have been in business
6. The number of people they employ
7. Peripheral businesses such as maintenance, landscaping, snow removal, etc.

8. The length of the management contract
9. Whether the contract is renewed automatically
10. Whether termination without cause is included
11. If the management company attends all meetings
12. The procedure the management company uses for handling emergency calls
13. The collection procedure for owner assessments
14. Whether financial management, such as budget preparation and financial reporting, is part of the management company's service
15. The amount of bond and/or insurance the company carries on its employees
16. The amount of the management fee
17. The cost of assistance in the sale of a unit
18. How often they perform site inspections

## THE COLLECTION POLICY REVIEW

1. A complete description of the collection policy
2. The percentage of owners who are currently delinquent
3. Whether collection is pursued by an attorney, the Board of Directors, or the management company

## THE MEETING MINUTES REVIEW

1. Review annual and board minutes for the two (2) most recent consecutive years
2. Summary of information important to buyers and owners

## THE COMMITTEES REVIEW

A list of all committees and the current undertaking of each

## THE NEWSLETTERS REVIEW

1. How often they are published
2. Who publishes them
3. The kinds of information included in them

## THE MASTER INSURANCE POLICY REVIEW

1. Amount of Property coverage
2. Amount of Liability coverage
3. Amount of Medical Payments coverage
4. Amount of Directors & Officers coverage
5. Amount of Net Income coverage
6. Amount of Personnel coverage

## THE WELCOME PACKET REVIEW

1. A list of the contents
2. Whether there is a Welcome Committee
3. A list of events specifically intended to include and educate new owners

## THE FINANCIAL REVIEW

1. A statement that all bank accounts are in the name of the association and under the association's tax identification number.

2. The schedule for the preparation and frequency of the financial statements

3. The number of signers that are required on accounts payable checks

4. The procedure for "checks and balances" regarding who writes checks, who makes deposits, and who reconciles the bank account(s)

5. A statement of budget amounts vs. actual expenses for the last fiscal year

6. A copy of the independent CPA audit for the last fiscal year

7. A copy of the most current month's balance sheet

8. A copy of the most current month's profit and loss statement

## THE OPERATING BUDGET REVIEW

1. The period of time covered for each budget (usually one fiscal year)

2. The amount of the current monthly or annual assessment (maintenance fee)

3. A list of the services that are paid from the owners' assessments (maintenance fees)

4. The percentage of the owners' assessments (maintenance fees) that are put into the replacement (reserves) fund

## THE REPLACEMENT (RESERVES) FUND REVIEW

1. The current balance in the fund (shown on the balance sheet)

2. The frequency of funding (shown on the profit and loss statement)

3. When the last Reserve Study was completed
4. Whether the owners are fully funding the replacement (reserves) fund according to the Reserve Study

## THE INVESTMENTS REVIEW

1. A procedure for the overall investment strategy
2. The name of the investment advisor
3. Names of the insured institutions that hold the association's funds
4. The types of low-risk instruments being used and their interest rates
5. The type of liquid instruments being used and their interest rates

## THE SPECIAL ASSESSMENTS REVIEW

1. The amounts of all current special assessments (total and per unit)
2. The purposes of all current special assessments
3. The timeframe for payment of all current special assessments
4. The procedure for payment of special assessment balance when a unit sells
5. The date of the last special assessment
6. The amount of the last special assessment (total and per unit)
7. The purpose of the last special assessment
8. Timeframe for payment of the last special assessment
9. Future plans for special assessment(s)

## THE PHYSICAL PROPERTY REVIEW

1. The current total number of units
2. The number of units remaining to be built (if association is still under construction)
3. A list of the recreational facilities
4. Amounts of the fees for use of recreational facilities if not included in the regular assessment
5. Parking assignments for each unit
6. Guest parking arrangements
7. Location(s) for rubbish collection
8. A description of the security system
9. A copy of the Preventive Maintenance Schedule

## THE DECLARANT (DEVELOPER) REVIEW (FOR CONDOMINIUMS STILL UNDER CONSTRUCTION)

1. The number of years the declarant (developer) has been in business
2. A list of the other communities built by the same declarant (developer)
3. The name of the management company hired by the developer
4. Contents of the Declarant's (Developer's) Disclosure Package:
    a. Site plan indicating placement of all Units, common elements and facilities, landscaping, roadways, retaining walls, etc.
    b. Proposed Declaration
    c. Proposed Bylaws
    d. Proposed Management Contract

e. Proposed budget

f. Proposed Owner Assessment schedule

g. New home warranty program

---

Each of the documents deals with an important aspect of the community association. Even if you must delay your purchase for a few days, you will have peace of mind and confidence in your decision.

---

 *WHAT'S NEXT? The next chapter contains easy-to-use checklists for gathering information as you visit various community associations and talk to the associations' professionals.*

# KAY'S EXCLUSIVE CONDO BUYER'S CHECKLISTS

## ARTICLES OF INCORPORATION

Legal name of the property_____

Purpose of the corporation _____

Charter number _____     Date filed _____

State of Incorporation _____

Board of Directors? (yes/no)

Names of *Initial* Board Members_____

_____

## DECLARATION OF CONDOMINIUM OWNERSHIP

Date filed _____     Name of the association_____

State _____

Name of the Declarant (Developer) _____

Location of property: _____     County _____

City/Township _____

Construction—circle all that apply: (masonry, brick, wood, aluminum siding, vinyl siding, stucco)

# of units _____

Still under development? (yes/no)

# of units when complete _____

# of buildings _____

Unit Style (single/double story) _____

Basement? (yes/no)

Unit entries (common/individual)

Attached garage? (yes/no)

Single _____    Double _____

# of parking spaces for this unit _____

# of guest parking spaces _____

Location of owner parking _____

Location of guest parking _____

Percentage of Ownership—this unit _____

Are percentages for all units *equal* or *different?* _____

Recreational Facilities (such as swimming pool, tennis courts, etc.): _____

Portions of the property *owned by the association* (such as foundations, roofs, roads, driveways, utility lines, etc.—**found under Common Elements & Facilities**):

_____

_____

_____

Portions of the property *owned by the unit owners* (such as interior walls, doors, utility lines, patio, balcony, etc.—**found under Limited Common Elements & Facilities**):

_____

_____

_____

Portions of the property that are the *association's responsibility to maintain and/or replace* (**found under Mgmt., Maintenance, Repairs & Replacement of Common Elements & Facilities—Responsibility of the Association**):

_____

_____

_____

Portions of the property that are the *unit owners' responsibility to maintain and/or replace* (**found under Mgmt., Maintenance, Repairs & Replacement of Common Elements & Facilities—Responsibility of the Owner**):

_____

_____

_____

## Restrictions for Architecture, Use, and Occupancy:

What items are permitted to be attached to building exteriors?

_____

Is owner responsible for common area damage by their
tenant(s) and guest(s)? (yes/no)

What type(s) of vehicles are NOT permitted on the property?

_____

What type(s) of vehicle repairs are permitted on the property?

_____

Animals: # permitted _____     Wt. restriction _____

Designated pet walking areas? (yes/no)

Type(s) of animals permitted _____

Resident age restriction _____     Leasing permitted? (yes/no)

Sale/Rent signs permitted? (yes/no)

Penalty for excessive noise? (yes/no) _____

Is business in unit permitted? (yes/no)

Are window treatments restricted? (yes/no)

      If so, to what? _____

Are "play" areas defined? (yes/no)   If yes, where?_____

Are laundry facilities defined? (yes/no)_____

Storage location for personal property (locker, special room, separate building, etc.)

    Other_____

Are changes permitted to:

    Fences? (yes/no)   Decks/Patios/Balconies? (yes/no)
    Landscaping? (yes/no)

What type(s) of recreational equipment and vehicles are owners permitted to have and where?

_____

_____

Prohibited activities _____

_____

OTHER _____

_____

Is there an architectural approval procedure? (yes/no)

    If so, what is it? _____

           _____

Due date for assessments (annually, monthly) _____

    Grace period _____

Penalties for non-payment and late payments (such as late fees, interest, loss of privileges, etc.):

_____

_____

_____

Penalties for failure to comply with Use and Occupancy Restrictions (such as violation fees, loss of privileges):

_____

_____

_____

Percentage of entire ownership needed to amend the Declaration _____

OTHER _____

_____

## BYLAWS

Date filed _____    Volume _____    Page(s) _____

Legal name of the association _____

Voting rights:   Percentage of Ownership _____

Each unit has one (1) Vote _____

Annual Meeting:    When is it held? _____

Is Proxy voting permitted? (yes/no) _____

Is a Nominating Committee required for election of Board Members? (yes/no)

Quorum requirement for Annual and
Special Meetings: _____

Board member requirements:    number of board members ____

Can non-owners serve on the board? (yes/no)

Can non-resident owners serve on the board? (yes/no)

Can spouses of owners serve on the board even if they are not owners? (yes/no)

How often are regular Board of Directors meetings to be scheduled?    Monthly _____          Bi-monthly _____
                    Quarterly _____          Semi-annually _____
                    Annually _____

Are regular Board of Directors meetings open to the unit owners? (yes/no)

Is the board permitted to have Executive Session meetings that are closed to owners? (yes/no)

If so, for what purpose(s)? _____

The Board of Directors has the following powers and duties:

| | Yes | No |
|---|---|---|
| Adopt and publish rules without owner consent | ____ | ____ |
| Declare the office of a member of the board to be vacant | ____ | ____ |
| Prepare and adopt the annual budget | ____ | ____ |
| Fix/notify unit owners of assessments for the common expenses | ____ | ____ |
| Establish/enforce methods of collecting assessments | ____ | ____ |
| Collect owners' assessments and make deposits | ____ | ____ |
| Provide for the operation and maintenance of the property | ____ | ____ |
| Pay for the cost of services out of the common assessments | ____ | ____ |
| Contract for repairs/additions/improvements after a catastrophe | ____ | ____ |
| Obtain/pay for insurance on the common elements | ____ | ____ |
| Enforce the provisions of the Declaration, Bylaws and rules | ____ | ____ |
| Notify owners of litigation against the association | ____ | ____ |
| Keep books with detailed accounts of receipts and expenses | ____ | ____ |
| Borrow money for repair/replacement of common elements | ____ | ____ |
| Delegate duties to firms, person, corporations | ____ | ____ |

OTHER _____

_____

_____


Duties of the officers of the Board of Directors (circle all that apply):

President:      (CEO, preside at meetings, sign legal
                documents/contracts, ensure board
                decisions are implemented)

                Other _____

Vice Pres.:     (take president's place in his absence)

                Other _____

Secretary:      (record votes, keep minutes of meetings,
                serve notices, maintain owner roster)

                Other _____

Treasurer:      (responsible for funds, keep records show-
                ing receipts/disbursements, prepare re-
                quired data, deposit funds, sign checks
                and promissory notes)

                Other _____

Are there any mandatory committees? (yes/no)

If so, what are they? _____

Can board appoint other committees? (yes/no)

The association has the following powers (usually exercised by the Board of Directors) for the benefit of all unit owners:

|  | Yes | No |
| --- | --- | --- |
| Purchase Casualty insurance for the common elements | ____ | ____ |
| Purchase Liability insurance for owners and occupants for injury, death, etc. arising from common elements | ____ | ____ |
| Purchase Directors & Officers Liability for slander, libel and gross negligence | ____ | ____ |
| Purchase Workers' Compensation insurance | ____ | ____ |
| Pay wages/fees for management, maintenance, legal counsel, accounting services, and the operation and enforcement of the Declaration and Bylaws | ____ | ____ |
| Pay for all the care of common elements and facilities | ____ | ____ |
| Pay any additional expenses to maintain the property as a first-class condominium property | ____ | ____ |
| Enter units to repair items that are association's responsibility | ____ | ____ |
| Notify owners of capital additions/improvements | ____ | ____ |

OTHER _____

_____

How often is the budget prepared? _____

When must owners be notified? _____

Must budget include reserves for contingencies/replacements? (yes/no)

Must owner pay his portion of common assessment if board fails or is late in preparing budget? (yes/no)

Are owners ever exempt from payment of assessments? (yes/no)

At end of fiscal year, is excess credited or shortage added to owners' accounts? (yes/no)

Is an annual audit by a CPA required? (yes/no)

Percentage of entire ownership needed to amend the Bylaws _____

OTHER _____

_____

## AMENDMENTS

Date filed _____    Volume _____

Page(s) _____    # of Amend. _____

Summary of Amendment content _____

_____

_____

Date filed _____    Volume _____

Page(s) _____    # of Amend. _____

Summary of Amendment content _____

_____

_____

Date filed _____        Volume _____

Page(s) _____        # of Amend. _____

Summary of Amendment content _____

_____

_____


# RULES, REGULATIONS AND/OR RESOLUTIONS

## Pets

Must be leashed when outside? (yes/no)

Length of leash _____        "Staking" permitted? (yes/no)

Pet "housing" permitted? (yes/no)

Designated pet walking area? (yes/no)

Can association remove pet for unreasonable disturbance or safety reasons upon notice? (yes/no)

If yes, how many days' and what type of notice? _____

## Parking

Is street parking permitted? (yes/no)

If yes, what are the time restrictions? _____

Are unit parking areas assigned? (yes/no)

Is guest parking designated?_____

# of vehicles permitted to park in unit's driveway _____

Can vehicles be towed? (yes/no)

    If so, for what reason(s) can they be towed?_____

Are vehicle repairs permitted? (yes/no)

    If yes, what location? _____

If owners have company vehicles, can they park them on the property? (yes/no)

## Rubbish Removal

How is rubbish collected? (dumpster, individual container)

Is recycling available? (yes/no)

Pick-up location for trash disposal (dumpster, container at end of driveway)

Is rubbish removed by the city/township/county for free? (yes/no)

    If no, is fee included in maintenance fee or paid directly to contractor by owners?_____

## Utilities

Which utilities are included in the maintenance fee?_____

Which utilities does the owner pay directly? _____

## Leasing

Is leasing of owners' units permitted? (yes/no)

If so, what are the restrictions and procedures? _____

_____

## Satellite Dish

Is satellite service provided by the association? (yes/no)

If no, are individual dishes permitted? (yes/no)

If yes, location(s) _____

## Signs

Are sale, rent and open house signs permitted? (yes/no)

If yes, location and times _____

Are patriotic, political and religious signs permitted? (yes/no)

If yes, which ones?_____

## Recreation

Are play areas designated? (yes/no)

If yes, where? _____

What type(s) of recreational equipment is permitted? _____

_____

Where must owners store this equipment? _____

_____

## Recreational Facilities

If there is a Club House, is there an extra fee for use or is usage included in the maintenance fee?

Included in maintenance fee **OR** Extra    $ _____

If there is a swimming pool, is there an extra fee for use or is usage included in the maintenance fee?

Included in maintenance fee **OR** Extra    $ _____

If there is a tennis court, is there an extra fee for use or is usage included in the maintenance fee?

Included in maintenance fee **OR** Extra    $ _____

If there is a basketball court, is there an extra fee for use or is usage included in the maintenance fee?

Included in maintenance fee **OR** Extra    $ _____

## Decorations

Which holiday(s) decorations are permitted to be attached to the exterior of the buildings?

_____

Timeframe for installation and removal of holiday decorations:

_____

What type(s) of flags are permitted? _____

Where can they be placed? _____

What kind of door decorations are permitted? _____

What kind of shrub bed decorations are permitted?

_____

Are bird feeders permitted? (yes/no)

How much are the violation fees?

    Pets _____    Parking _____    Trash _____

    Signs _____    Decorations _____

What is the Complaint Procedure? _____

_____

_____


## MANAGEMENT COMPANY

Name of the Company _____    Phone _____

Street, State, Zip _____

Is the company incorporated? (yes/no)

Is the contract for full or partial service? (full/partial)

    If partial, what part(s)? _____

Has the company been appointed as the <u>exclusive</u> agent to manage the property? (yes/no)

What is the term of the contract?_____

Will it <u>automatically</u> renew? (yes/no)

    If yes, for how long? _____

Can the company be terminated with or without
cause? (with, without)

    With how much time and what form of notice? _____

    _____

    _____

Are the company and its employees insured and bonded and
for how much? _____

How long has the company managed the association? _____

How long in business? _____

What credentials/designations does the company have? _____

_____

What credentials/designations does the manager have? _____

_____

How many employees? _____

What peripheral businesses such as maintenance, landscaping,
snow removal, etc. does the company own? _____

_____

How many association/board meetings will the management
company attend per year? _____

What is the base management fee?_____

What is the charge for meeting attendance? _____

For what functions can the company charge extra, in addition to the base management fee and how much (such as record storage, copies, postage, bidding, correspondence, etc.)?

_____

_____

_____

What is the chain of response for emergencies? _____

_____

What <u>financial</u> duties does the company perform on behalf of the association?

Budget Prep _____     Financial Reports _____

Collect maintenance fees _____     Pay bills _____

File liens/foreclosures _____

Prepare tax return _____

What are the limits of liability and indemnification the association must carry on the agent? _____

_____

_____

Is the company expected to perform property inspections of the common elements? (yes/no)

If so, how often? _____

Is the company expected to oversee/monitor performance of contractors and employees? (yes/no)

How much does the company charge for assistance in the sale of a unit?_____

Is the contract assignable without association permission? (yes/no)

OTHER _____

_____

_____

_____

_____

_____

## MEETING MINUTES, COMMITTEES, NEWSLETTERS AND WELCOME PACKET

### Meeting Minutes

It is a good idea to review the minutes of regular Board of Directors and Annual meetings for the last couple of years. Meeting minutes will disclose the following information:

|  | Yes | No |
|---|---|---|
| Are the Board of Directors meetings regularly held? | ____ | ____ |
| Has an annual meeting been held each year? | ____ | ____ |
| Have board members been elected at each annual meeting? | ____ | ____ |
| Are the following activities indicated in the minutes? | | |
|     Parliamentary procedure used, i.e., use of motions | ____ | ____ |
|     Prior meeting minutes read and approved | ____ | ____ |

|  | Yes | No |
|---|---|---|
| Financial reports given | ____ | ____ |
| Delinquency reports given | ____ | ____ |
| Reports from committees | ____ | ____ |
| Reports from the management company | ____ | ____ |
| Reports from independent contractors | ____ | ____ |
| Reports from Declarant (if new association) | ____ | ____ |
| Discussion of bids received | ____ | ____ |
| Decisions made about property maintenance | ____ | ____ |
| Decisions made about recreational facilities | ____ | ____ |
| Decisions and/or discussions about owners' issues | ____ | ____ |
| Residents forum (time for owners to speak) | ____ | ____ |
| Do board members have unity when making decisions? | ____ | ____ |
| **Are there any discussions that would indicate an increase in the assessments (maintenance fees) or a special assessment?** | ____ | ____ |

## Committees

|  | Yes | No |
|---|---|---|
| What committees are in existence? |  |  |
| Nominations Committee | ____ | ____ |
| Elections Committee | ____ | ____ |
| Architectural Standards Committee | ____ | ____ |
| Finance/Budget Committee | ____ | ____ |

|  | Yes | No |
|---|---|---|
| Grounds/Landscaping Committee | ____ | ____ |
| Social Committee | ____ | ____ |
| Welcome Committee | ____ | ____ |
| Newsletter Committee | ____ | ____ |
| Recreation Committee | ____ | ____ |
| Public Relations Committee | ____ | ____ |
| Rules Committee | ____ | ____ |
| Dispute Resolution Committee | ____ | ____ |
| Communications Committee | ____ | ____ |

## Newsletters

How often are they published?   (Monthly, Bi-Monthly, Quarterly, Semi-Annually, Annually)

Who publishes them?   (Owner, Committee, Board of Directors, Management Company)

|  | Yes | No |
|---|---|---|
| What type of information is contained in the Newsletters? |  |  |
| Social events | ____ | ____ |
| Trips | ____ | ____ |
| Pictures (residents, activities, property) | ____ | ____ |
| Calendar of events | ____ | ____ |
| Reports from the Board of Directors | ____ | ____ |
| Financial information (budgets, assessments, etc.) | ____ | ____ |

|  | Yes | No |
|---|---|---|
| Reports from committees | ___ | ___ |
| "Thank You" articles for volunteer workers | ___ | ___ |
| Units for sale or rent | ___ | ___ |
| Results of owner surveys | ___ | ___ |
| Notices of maintenance work on the property | ___ | ___ |
| Rule reminders | ___ | ___ |
| News about residents (marriages, births, deaths, etc.) | ___ | ___ |
| Classifieds | ___ | ___ |
| Advertisements by contractors and/or professionals | ___ | ___ |
| Civic events | ___ | ___ |
| Directory of civic and association phone numbers | ___ | ___ |

## Welcome Packet

Who is responsible to welcome new residents? (Board of Directors, Committee, residents)

|  | Yes | No |
|---|---|---|
| What type of information is included in the Welcome Packet? | | |
| Names, addresses, phone numbers, emails for current members of the Board of Directors | ___ | ___ |
| Name, address, phone, email of the management co. | ___ | ___ |

|                                                      | Yes | No |
|------------------------------------------------------|-----|-----|
| Roster of owners and residents                       | ___ | ___ |
| Recent newsletters                                   | ___ | ___ |
| Notice of upcoming meetings                          | ___ | ___ |
| Calendar of events                                   | ___ | ___ |
| List of Committees and their current reports         | ___ | ___ |
| Directory of civic and association phone numbers     | ___ | ___ |
| Coupons from area vendors                            | ___ | ___ |
| Food item and/or flowers                             | ___ | ___ |

## FINANCIAL

### Operating Budget

What period of time does the Operating Budget cover? _____

_____

Who prepares the Operating Budget?   (Board of Directors, Finance Committee, Management Company)?

What is the <u>annual</u> assessment (maintenance fee) for this unit?

_____

Is annual payment of the assessment (maintenance fee) <u>mandatory?</u> (yes/no)

What is the <u>monthly</u> assessment (maintenance fee) for this unit?

_____

Do all units pay the same assessment (maintenance fee)?
(yes/no)

What services are paid for from the owners' assessments (**found
in the Expense section of the Operating Budget**)?

_____

_____

_____

_____

_____

_____

_____

The total amount of money that is budgeted annually to be put
into the Replacement (Reserves) Fund from the owners' assessments (maintenance fees)? _____

## Replacement (Reserves) Fund

How much is <u>currently</u> in the Replacement (Reserves) Fund
(shown on the **Balance Sheet**)?

$ _____

How often is it funded (shown on the **Profit & Loss Statement**)?
(Monthly, Quarterly, Semi-Annually, Annually)

When was the last Reserve Study completed? _____

By whom?_____

How long has the Reserve Study company been
in business? _____

Is the association fully funding the Replacement (Reserves) Fund according to the Reserve Study? (yes/no)

## Investments

Name and address of the professional investment advisor

_____

Is there a procedure for the overall investment strategy of the association? (yes/no)

Names of the institutions that hold the association's funds, whether they are insured, whether the funds are liquid and the interest rates for each account:

| Name | Insured (y/n) | Liquid (y/n) | Interest Rate |
|------|---------------|--------------|---------------|
|      |               |              |               |
|      |               |              |               |
|      |               |              |               |
|      |               |              |               |

## Special Assessments

All <u>current</u> special assessments:

| Purpose | Total Amount | Amount/ Unit | Payment Period |
|---------|--------------|--------------|----------------|
|         |              |              |                |
|         |              |              |                |

<u>Last two (2)</u> special assessments:

| Purpose | Total Amount | Amount/ Unit | Payment Period |
|---|---|---|---|
| | | | |
| | | | |

<u>Future</u> plans for special assessments:

| Purpose | Total Amount | Amount/ Unit | Payment Period |
|---|---|---|---|
| | | | |
| | | | |

Who pays the balance due on a special assessment when the unit is sold? (Seller/Buyer)

## Collection Policy

When are common assessment (maintenance fee) payments due?

_____

Is there a grace period? (yes/no)   If yes, what is it? _____

What is the penalty for non-payment or late payment? _____

Is there an administrative late charge by the <u>association</u> for any late payment and on any unpaid balance? (yes/no)

   If yes, what is it? _____

Is there an administrative late charge by the <u>management company</u> for any check returned for insufficient funds or for any other reason?   If yes, what is it?_____

Is a collection letter sent <u>without any other type of notice</u> to an owner whose maintenance fee is delinquent? (yes/no)

At what amount of delinquency is a lien filed against an account? _____

Once the delinquency is paid, when is the lien released so the title is cleared?_____

At what amount of delinquency is foreclosure action taken?

_____

Once the delinquency is paid, when is the foreclosure dismissed so the title is cleared? _____

Which of the above actions are performed by the board, an attorney or the management company and how much do they cost?

|                    | Board | Attorney | Mgmt. Co. | Cost |
|--------------------|-------|----------|-----------|------|
| Collection letter  | _____ | _____    | _____     | _____ |
| Lien filing        | _____ | _____    | _____     | _____ |
| Foreclosure filing | _____ | _____    | _____     | _____ |

Are any of these three (3) costs added to the owner's account? (yes/no)

　　If so, which one(s)? _____

_____

Any payments made by the owner are typically applied in the following order:

a) Administrative late fees owed to the Association

b) Collection costs, attorney's fees incurred by the Association

c) Principal amounts owed on the account for common expenses and assessments

Is the above payment application correct for this association? (yes/no)

If no, what is the application order? _____

_____

_____

_____

When was the collection procedure adopted by the board?

_____

What is the percentage of owners who are currently delinquent (**compare number of delinquent owners to number of total owners**)? _____

## General Financial

How often are financial statements prepared? (Monthly, Quarterly, Semi-Annually, Annually)

Who prepares them? (Board of Directors, Management Company, Accountant)

Are the association's bank accounts all separate from each other? (yes/no)

Are the association's bank accounts all separate from any other condominium association's accounts? (yes/no)

Are the association's bank accounts in the name and tax number of the association? (yes/no)

How many signers are required on each association account? _____

Who are the signers and are they board members and/or management company agents?

| Name | Board | Mgmt. Co. |
| --- | --- | --- |
| | | |
| | | |
| | | |
| | | |
| | | |
| | | |
| | | |

Can the same person who reconciles the bank accounts be a check signer? (yes/no)

Can the same person who reconciles the bank accounts make deposits? (yes/no)

Did the association's Profit & Loss statement for the last year agree with the budget for the last year? (yes/no)

I have received a copy of the most current month's Balance
Sheet:   yes _____     no _____

I have received a copy of the most current month's Profit &
Loss statement:   yes _____     no _____


# INSURANCE, PHYSICAL PROPERTY AND DECLARANT (DEVELOPER)

## Insurance

What period of time does current insurance policy cover?

_____

Who is the underwriter (insurance company), who is the agent
and where is the agent located?

Underwriter _____

Agent_____

Agent's Address _____

_____

Does the association have a Risk Management Program (not to
be confused with the association's insurance policy)? (yes/no)

What is the amount of the association's **Property**
coverage?   $ _____

What is the amount of the association's **Liability**
coverage?   $ _____

What is the amount of the association's **Medical Payments**
coverage?   $ _____

What is the amount of the association's **Directors & Officers**
coverage?   $ _____

## Physical Property

What is the total number of units currently? _____

Will more units be built (if the association is still under construction)? (yes/no)

    If so, how many? _____

    When is the development scheduled to be completed?

    _____

How old is the condominium property? _____

Has the Board of Directors or management company prepared
a Preventive Maintenance Schedule? (yes/no)

When was the last property inspection performed by the Board
of Directors and/or the management company? _____

How often are property inspections done and
by whom? _____

Is the property in a low-crime area? (yes/no)

Is the unit in a desirable location within the condominium
property? (yes/no)

Is the unit close to good schools? (yes/no)

Does the association have a particular "draw" such as a beach/lake, progressive downtown district or desirable suburban location? (yes/no)

    If yes, what? _____

Does the surrounding residential setting have a good mix of single family and apartments? (yes/no)

Is there easy access to freeways, mass transit and airports? (yes/no)

    If yes, what? _____

Are shopping and recreation close by? (yes/no)

Does it have good "curb appeal"? (yes/no)

Is the development located on a busy street? (yes/no)

Is the unit near garages or carports where cars are constantly coming and going? (yes/no)

Are the units spread far apart, allowing for some degree of privacy? (yes/no)

Do you have to walk around several other units to get to your unit? (yes/no)

Is there ample lighting from windows, doors and skylights? (yes/no)

Does the unit have modern appliances? (yes/no)

Does the unit have modern decorating? (yes/no)

Is the unit large enough for you to enjoy and still command a reasonable price for a quick resale later? (yes/no)

Does the interior layout seem logical or awkward?

## Declarant (Developer)—if new development

Name of the Declarant _____

      Address _____

              _____

How long has the Declarant been in business? _____

Is he the original Developer of the property? (yes/no)

A list of other associations built by this Declarant:

| Name | Address |
| --- | --- |
|  |  |
|  |  |
|  |  |
|  |  |
|  |  |
|  |  |

If there is currently a management company, were they hired by the Declarant? (yes/no)

The following items were contained in the Declarant's (Developer's) Disclosure Package:

|  | Yes | No |
|---|---|---|
| Site Plan | _____ | _____ |
| Proposed Declaration | _____ | _____ |
| Proposed Bylaws | _____ | _____ |
| Proposed Management Contract | _____ | _____ |
| Proposed Budget | _____ | _____ |
| Proposed Owner Assessment Schedule | _____ | _____ |
| New Home Warranty Program | _____ | _____ |

## ASK THE RESIDENTS!

One of the best ways to get the "flavor" of the community is to talk to those who live there. Feel free to knock on several doors, tell them you are a prospective buyer and you have some questions. *Regardless of what the governing documents and rules say, you want to find out what living in this community is like directly from those who live there.*

Address _____    Style of Unit _____

How long have you lived here? _____

Are you glad you purchased your unit? (yes/no)

    Why or why not? _____

    _____

Address_____     Style of Unit _____

How long have you lived here? _____

Are you glad you purchased your unit? (yes/no)

    Why or why not? _____

    _____


Address_____     Style of Unit _____

How long have you lived here? _____

Are you glad you purchased your unit? (yes/no)

    Why or why not? _____

    _____


What is the age group of most of the residents? _____

Is anything different than you thought it would be? _____

    _____


Have you experienced any "surprises" while living here? _____

    If so, what kind? _____

    _____

    _____


Are there planned social events? (yes/no)

    If so, what kind? _____

    _____

    _____

Does the association have its own employees? (yes/no)

If so, what kind? _____

_____

Has there been any vandalism or other crime? (yes/no)

If so, what kind? _____

_____

## General

|  | Yes | No |
| --- | --- | --- |
| Is there a play area for children? | ____ | ____ |
| Are the recreational facilities in good condition? | ____ | ____ |
| Is it a quiet community? | ____ | ____ |
| Are the residents friendly? | ____ | ____ |

## Financial

|  | Yes | No |
| --- | --- | --- |
| Has there been a special assessment since you've lived here? | ____ | ____ |
| If so, did you think it was for a good reason? | ____ | ____ |
| If so, did you like the payment options? | ____ | ____ |
| Have the assessments (maintenance fees) gone up every year? | ____ | ____ |
| Have the units appreciated in value? | ____ | ____ |

| | Yes | No |
|---|---|---|

## Board

Is there good communication from the Board? ____ ____

Do you know what's going on in the community? ____ ____

Do you think the rules are fair and consistently enforced? ____ ____

Are your questions answered promptly? ____ ____

Are your complaints resolved quickly? ____ ____

## Management Company

Do you like how the property is being managed? ____ ____

Are the company's employees friendly? ____ ____

Do you always get a "live" person when you call? ____ ____

Are your phone calls returned within a satisfactory time period? ____ ____

Do you receive violation letters from them? ____ ____

Are your issues taken care of promptly? ____ ____

Do you like the property manager? ____ ____

## Pets

Are there many pets? ____ ____

Are pets walked on leashes? ____ ____

|                                                      | Yes  | No   |
| ---------------------------------------------------- | ---- | ---- |
| Is staking or tying out of pets permitted?           | ____ | ____ |
| Is there a designated pet walking area?              | ____ | ____ |
| Is pet soiling cleaned up promptly?                  | ____ | ____ |

## Parking

|                                                      | Yes  | No   |
| ---------------------------------------------------- | ---- | ---- |
| Is resident parking sufficient?                      | ____ | ____ |
| Is guest parking sufficient?                         | ____ | ____ |
| Are vehicles often towed off the property?           | ____ | ____ |

## Maintenance

|                                                      | Yes  | No   |
| ---------------------------------------------------- | ---- | ---- |
| Are you satisfied with the landscaper?               | ____ | ____ |
| Are you satisfied with the snow removal contractor?  | ____ | ____ |
| Are maintenance issues resolved quickly?             | ____ | ____ |

## Meetings

|                                                      | Yes  | No   |
| ---------------------------------------------------- | ---- | ---- |
| Do you go to board meetings?                         | ____ | ____ |
| Are owners permitted to speak?                       | ____ | ____ |
| Are owners treated with respect at the meetings?     | ____ | ____ |
| Are board meetings well run?                         | ____ | ____ |
| Do board members have unity when making decisions?   | ____ | ____ |

|                                                    | Yes  | No   |
| -------------------------------------------------- | ---- | ---- |

## Declarant (Developer)

Is the declarant still involved on the property?    \_\_\_\_    \_\_\_\_

If so, do the residents get along well with him?    \_\_\_\_    \_\_\_\_

Does the declarant honor his warranties?    \_\_\_\_    \_\_\_\_

> *You can download these checklists from our website in 8.5 × 11 inch format.*
>
> www.condo-condominium.com

# WHY SHOULD I GET INVOLVED IN THE ASSOCIATION?

*Protect your investment!*

You do not have to take on a full-time job to protect your investment and have a positive influence in the community.

The owners, a young, newly married couple who were both professionals, loved their condominium. It was exactly the carefree lifestyle that suited their busy schedules. Additionally, their unit was at the end of the property, so it was very quiet, which they also liked. All of a sudden, things changed. There was a ground-breaking ceremony for a putt-putt golf course right across the street from their unit. How did this happen without their knowledge? As they soon discovered, this recreational facility had been under discussion for the last year. In fact, an owner survey was taken to ascertain the owners' opinions, not only about the facility but about the Declaration Amendment and the special assessment it was going to take to make it happen. Because they were rarely home, they weren't contacted about the survey. According to the Declaration, it only took 75% of the owners to approve this, so their vote wasn't needed. Because they never attended association meetings, they didn't know the association was considering a special assessment.

When you buy a home, it is usually one of the largest financial investments you make. Therefore, you want to protect and enhance that investment. Even though that may be the goal, there is an added dimension to your purchase. The decision to live in a condominium is different from other residential purchases you can make.

- As a member of the association, you are not only the owner of a unit, but you are co-owner of a business. Therefore, your responsibility is greater than just owning your own home.
- You have the responsibility of helping the community become everything it can be—in safety, aesthetics, and financial value. This does not mean you have to become a board or committee member, but you should make every effort to know what is going on and give input to the association leaders when possible.

## YOU WILL HAVE QUESTIONS

If you have decided to live in a community association, you probably have a vision of how you would like your condo and the property in general to look. You may also have thoughts about whether it is a safe environment and wonder how changes are made. You may have questions about these issues, and more. Therefore, you need to know how and where to get your questions answered and your concerns resolved.

## HAVE THE PROPER PERSPECTIVE

One of the universal phrases in an association's governing documents is "to protect, preserve, and enhance" the community. This means that the needs of the community must be looked at and managed objectively, with an eye toward its future. A well-run association identifies, builds, and acts upon the ideas of its residents and the input of professionals.

Owners with the correct perspective do not look at the needs of a particular individual; they look at what is best for the entire community. They consider how each decision will affect the property and living conditions of all association members. They see the services the association provides as a way of satisfying the residents and making the condominium complex a better place to live.

## HOW TO BE INVOLVED IN A POSITIVE WAY

- ☺ Join a committee—condominium associations may have committees that would interest you, such as Social, Welcoming, Finance, etc.
- ☺ Become a board member—serving on the Board of Directors in your condominium association gives you the opportunity to be part of the decision-making process that affects the entire community.
- ☺ Edit, co-edit, or write an article for the association's newsletter—help keep members informed about the board's decisions and events in the community.
- ☺ Attend social events—get to know your neighbors, share your concerns and ideas, and have fun!
- ☺ Take part in the welcoming of new members—new members will be more likely to be helpful and less

likely to be confused after receiving a warm welcome and useful information.

☺ Participate in owner surveys—help committee and board members develop future plans.

☺ Get to know those in the community—your neighbors will be happy to have new friends!

☺ Ask questions—the association's leaders will be happy to share information.

☺ Attend seminars—learn more about residing in and leading a community association.

☺ Attend and participate in meetings—your votes and opinions count!

## A FEW WAYS TO MAKE ENEMIES!

☹ Make as much noise as you feel like at any time of the day or night.

☹ Stop paying your maintenance fees because the snow removal company skipped your driveway.

☹ Park your vehicle in someone else's spot.

☹ Yell at the Board of Directors because the maintenance fees went up.

☹ Tell everyone the management company is crooked because they charge for their services.

☹ Get upset because a repair wasn't done as quickly as you wanted.

☹ Let your pet run without a leash.

☹ Don't clean up after your pet soils.

## BIG REWARDS!

Depending on your level of involvement, you have the opportunity to:

- ☺ Protect your investment.
- ☺ Influence vital management decisions.
- ☺ Encourage harmony among residents.
- ☺ Contribute time and energy toward the association's management.
- ☺ Promote communication between all parties.

> Associations are in need of different levels of involvement from their owners. Many areas of participation offer the opportunity to be creative and have fun!

*WHAT'S NEXT? Finding time to attend meetings may be difficult. In the next chapter, we will discuss why they are so important.*

# ARE ASSOCIATION MEETINGS IMPORTANT?

Communication—how does it happen?

Requests—how do they get implemented?

Questions—how do they get answered?

*If the association fails to conduct efficient meetings, owners may lose confidence in the Board of Directors and the management company.*

Your rights and obligations as a homeowner and a member of the association include attending meetings and participating in the community. In Florida, all meetings, with very limited exceptions, must be open to all members. Notice must be posted in a conspicuous place at least 48 hours before a meeting or 7 days if by mail, except in an emergency. Further, Florida law mandates that the association is required to hold an annual meeting, open to all members. Without question, most homeowners have busy schedules. Finding the time to attend meetings and to take an active role in the community is difficult. However, failure to participate can leave you at the mercy of a rogue board.

**Q WHAT KIND OF MEETINGS DOES AN ASSOCIATION HAVE?**

- Annual
- Special
- Organizational
- Regular Board Meetings
- Executive Sessions

**Q WHAT IS THE PURPOSE OF THE ANNUAL MEETING?**

A   A community association operates as a business, even if it is not incorporated. Therefore, it must conduct meetings of its "shareholders"—the owners.

A   Annual Meetings provide a forum for owners to elect a Board of Directors from among themselves, who will manage the community and conduct its affairs. Note that owners elect members to the Board of Directors, but they do not elect officers. See the description of the Organizational Meeting that follows.

A   The Annual Meeting also brings owners together to take any action delegated to them by the governing documents.

A   The owners have a right to vote based on their percentage of ownership in the association.

A   The Annual Meeting is also like the "State of the Union" for the association. The Board of Directors and other professionals (management company, attorney, accountant, etc.) who serve the association should make their respective reports regarding the health of the association.

A Typically, the *Bylaws* for the association state the criteria for the Annual Meeting, including meeting notice, quorum, voting, and proxy procedures.

A The owners may attend in person or by proxy, unless proxy use is prohibited by statute.

A Notification must be given to all owners stating the time, date, and place of the meeting. This notice must be distributed in the time allotted by statute and the governing documents.

## Q WHAT IS THE PURPOSE OF A SPECIAL MEETING?

A A Special Meeting is the second type of owners' meeting. It provides a forum for *ONLY* the business that was stated in the meeting notice. Conducting business that is not indicated in the notice disenfranchises those who did not attend based upon what they were told would be the subject of the meeting.

A The Board of Directors may call a Special Meeting. Also, the *Bylaws* usually allow a group of owners to call a Special Meeting. Normally, a specified number of members sign a petition and present it to the board president or secretary. The petition must <u>precisely</u> state the purpose of the meeting and meet the percentage requirement of owners to call it. The president or secretary then calls the meeting for the purpose contained in the petition.

## Q WHAT IF THERE ISN'T A QUORUM FOR AN ANNUAL OR SPECIAL MEETING?

A The term quorum refers to the minimum number of owners that must be present, in person or by proxy, for the meeting to be official. This percentage is set by statute and in the *Bylaws*. If the quorum is not met, valid business cannot be transacted. The meeting must be adjourned and rescheduled for another date.

## Q   WHAT IS AN ORGANIZATIONAL MEETING?

A   Because the condominium association is a business, it must have officers to conduct its affairs. The Organizational Meeting is normally held within twenty-four (24) hours of the Annual Meeting. Its purpose is for the Board of Directors to elect its own officers. Officers are normally the president, vice president, secretary, and treasurer.

## Q   WHAT IS THE PURPOSE OF REGULAR BOARD MEETINGS?

A   Meetings of the Board of Directors are mandatory as stated in the governing documents of the association. In the Board of Directors section of the *Bylaws*, the time, place and number of board meetings per year will be listed. Occasionally, all of these requirements are left to the board's discretion, but normally at least quarterly meetings are required. Important decisions are made that impact the quality of life, enhance overall value of the community and the individual units, and set the boundaries within which management will function. Some of the types of decisions made at board meetings are:

- Approve prior meetings' minutes
- Determine work needed on common elements and facilities

- Decide on purchases of equipment, supplies, etc.
- Select contractors
- Discuss and determine action on owner requests and complaints
- Decide on delinquent assessment collection action
- Committee reports
- Management company report
- Receive the financial report

## Q WHAT IS AN EXECUTIVE SESSION?

A A Board of Directors Executive Session is only for board members—owners are prohibited from attending. There are times when a board discusses and makes decisions of a sensitive nature. Many states have "sunshine laws," which limit the reasons for a board to have closed or executive sessions. Some of the reasons for an Executive Session include discussions involving:

- Personnel issues
- Contract negotiations
- Lawsuits and other legal matters
- Investigative proceedings related to criminal activity
- Unit owner disciplinary hearings

## Q MAY I SPEAK AT MEETINGS?

A It is important to understand that Organizational and Executive Session Board meetings are for the board to make specific business decisions. Owners have no vote on the types of transactions that are decided at these two meetings. However, there are three different association meetings at which an owner may speak.

1. <u>The Annual Meeting</u>
   a. During the Annual Meeting, owners make ALL of the decisions.
   b. Owners elect board members.
   c. Owners may ask questions of the board and all the professionals present at the meeting.

2. <u>Special Meetings</u>
   a. Owners may ask questions of the board and all the professionals present at the meeting.
   b. If there is a decision to be made about the subject of the meeting, it may be one that requires owner input and vote.

3. <u>Regular Board Meetings</u>
   a. Board Meetings are usually closed to owner communication during their decision-making process.
   b. Most boards have an "open session" at some time during their meeting to allow owners to voice their concerns and ask questions.

 *Buyer's Tip—Stay informed! Attend the Board of Directors meetings. Even if there is no "open session" at which you can speak, you will still have knowledge of the board's decisions. Virtually all of their actions affect you!*

## Q ARE THERE MINUTES OF ASSOCIATION MEETINGS?

A There certainly should be! All meetings, even those of committees, should have official minutes. Minutes contain decisions made during the meeting and provide permanent proof of positions and actions taken. Minutes of meetings (other than Executive Session) should be <u>public knowledge</u> and include the following information:

- Type of meeting—Annual, Special, Board, Committee, etc.
- Name of the association
- Date, time, and place of the meeting
- Presence of the president or chairperson and recording secretary
- Presence of a quorum, if necessary
- Names of those in attendance
- Action taken on the minutes of the previous meeting and corrections, if any
- Exact wording of each motion and name of person making and seconding it
- Facts about whether the motion was adopted, failed, or withdrawn
- Time of adjournment

---

Meetings are <u>absolutely</u> one of the main sources of communication between the owners, the management company (if there is one) and the Board of Directors.

**A well-run board will have well-managed, successful meetings.**

---

*WHAT'S NEXT? How do you know what the association expects from you? What can you expect from them?*

# WHAT ARE THE ASSOCIATION'S & OWNERS' RESPONSIBILITIES AND RIGHTS?

*The secret of a happy community!*

Community leaders and homeowners working together create harmony and prosperity.

The owners in a condominium association "heard" that there was going to be a special assessment. Because of the miscommunication, the owners believed what they heard and started a petition to remove the board members. When the board got wind of the petition, they scheduled an informational meeting with the owners. All of the owners' questions were answered at the meeting. In fact, the board had not yet levied the special assessment. The meeting was very well attended and all were cooperative in their attitudes. The owners were able to express their opinions about the possible future special assessment.

## ASSOCIATION RESPONSIBILITIES

The association's responsibilities, performed through its Board of Directors, fall into three main categories—administrative/legal, financial, and property.

1. Administrative/Legal
   a. Monitor day-to-day operation of the association.
   b. Keep correct and current records.
   c. Properly insure common elements and facilities.
   d. Conduct meetings required by the governing documents.
   e. Maintain an owner roster.
   f. Hire contractors and employees.
   g. Communicate with the owners.
   h. Fulfill fiduciary duties as required by the governing documents.
   i. Exercise sound business judgment.
   j. Disclose personal and financial conflicts of interest.

2. Financial
   a. Collect assessments from unit owners.
   b. Pay the association's expenses.
   c. Create the association's budgets.
   d. Prepare financial statements.
   e. Invest association assets.

3. Property
   a. Create preventive maintenance schedules for the common elements and facilities.
   b. Maintain, repair, and replace common elements and facilities in a timely fashion.

## ASSOCIATION LEADERS HAVE THE RIGHT TO:

1. Expect owners to meet their financial obligations to the community.
2. Count on residents to know and comply with the rules and resolutions.
3. Expect residents to be respectful and honest.
4. Receive support and constructive input from owners when requested.
5. Require owners to conduct themselves in a courteous manner at meetings.

## OWNERS' RESPONSIBILITIES

The unit owners' responsibilities fall into three main categories—communication, maintenance, and compliance.

1. Communication
   a. Notify leaders and/or managers of needed maintenance or replacement of common elements and facilities.
   b. Notify leaders and/or managers when selling or leasing their unit.
   c. Provide current contact information to association leaders and/or managers.
   d. Communicate their willingness to serve on a committee or on the board.
   e. Request permission from the board before making an architectural change to their unit or surrounding area.
   f. Encourage a harmonious atmosphere within the community.

2. <u>Maintenance</u>
    a. Maintain or replace those elements of their unit or property that are designated as owner responsibility in the governing documents.
    b. Maintain a homeowner's insurance policy.
    c. Avoid storing personal items on the common elements.
    d. Keep the area adjacent to the unit free of litter.

3. <u>Compliance</u>
    a. Obey all restrictions set forth in the governing documents and rules.
    b. Vote in community elections and on other issues.
    c. Pay association assessments and charges on time.
    d. Respect the rights of others within the community.
    e. Observe government laws/ordinances that apply to the condominium complex.

## OWNERS HAVE THE RIGHT TO:

1. Receive honest, fair and respectful treatment from the association's leaders and managers.

2. Participate in meetings, on committees, and on the Board of Directors.

3. Place their names into nomination for election to the board.

4. Access association records.

5. Receive the association's budgets and notices of payment due dates and amounts.

6. Expect association's leaders to expend association funds prudently.

7. Live in a community that is maintained according to established standards.

8. Receive a copy of all changes to the governing documents and rules.

9. Appeal any decision that seems unfair or discriminatory.

> When all parties dedicate themselves to the fulfillment of their responsibilities and the need to respect each other, the community is a pleasant place to live!

*WHAT'S NEXT? The next chapter discusses the roles of the board, committees, and officers. If you want to participate in the association, you will need to know the different levels of involvement available.*

# WHAT ARE THE RESPONSIBILITIES OF THE BOARD OF DIRECTORS, COMMITTEES, AND OFFICERS?

*Don't be frustrated!*

*Know who to ask for answers to your questions.*

Board of Directors

Committees

Officers

An association in Texas needed to replace the roofs on all of the units because the complex was 20 years old. The board realized this was a massive undertaking and met to discuss how to address the problem. There were many issues about which they needed information and all of the board members worked full-time jobs, so they decided to form ad hoc (temporary) committees of volunteer owners who had specific expertise in the areas needed for this project. Each committee was chaired by a board member. The committees were Roof Evaluation, Contractor Procurement, Project Funding, Project

Monitoring, and Communication. All committees completed their tasks and kept the owners informed of the progress from the beginning to the end of the project.

## BOARD OF DIRECTORS

State law defines a corporation and provides for the Board of Directors to be the governing body responsible for operating the corporation. When a declarant (developer) writes the governing documents for a community association, the restrictions and guidelines for the corporation are enumerated.

The Board of Directors bears the ultimate fiduciary duty for operating the community association on behalf of the owners. The board can delegate authority to act on its behalf but can NEVER delegate its responsibility to supervise the implementation of its decisions.

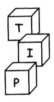

*Buyer's Tip—Even if an association is not incorporated, the Declaration and Bylaws will lay out the guidelines for the responsibilities and duties of the Board of Directors.*

## COMMITTEES

Mandatory committees are those required by the *Declaration* and *Bylaws*. Ad hoc committees may be permitted but are not defined in the governing documents. Ad hoc committees are formed at the request of the Board of Directors for specific purposes and lengths of time. Both kinds of committees typically consist of owners appointed by the Board of Directors.

Committees are a tremendous help to the board. They take on some of the legwork and research, which saves board members a great deal of time. Committees assist the board in meeting its responsibilities and serve the board in an advisory capacity.

 *Buyer's Tip—Volunteering for a committee is a proven way to be involved in the life of a community association. Owners don't feel frustrated when they have input on board decisions.*

**Q  WHAT ARE THE RESPONSIBILITIES OF THE BOARD OF DIRECTORS?**

**A**  Enforce compliance with the governing documents.

Establish standards and rules.

Create procedures for the maintenance of the common elements and facilities.

Create procedures for the operation of the association's business.

Monitor maintenance, social, and security programs.

Maintain and enhance the physical common elements and facilities.

Manage community finances and create the annual budget.

Develop a risk management program to protect the community's assets.

Manage employees and volunteers.

Preserve and promote community harmony.

**Q WHAT FUNCTIONS MIGHT A COMMITTEE PERFORM?**

**A** Gather owners' opinions and attitudes.

Train future board members.

Act as liaison between the board and owners.

Explain board actions to the community.

Research methods by which particular tasks can be accomplished.

Report all recommendations to the Board of Directors.

**Q WHAT ARE SOME TYPES OF MANDATORY COMMITTEES?**

**A** Elections

Nominations

Architectural standards

**Q WHAT ARE SOME TYPES OF AD HOC COMMITTEES?**

**A** Budget/Finance

Grounds

Social

Welcome

Newsletter

Recreation

Public Relations

Rules and Dispute Resolution

Communications

## Q WHO ARE THE OFFICERS AND WHAT ARE THEIR DUTIES?

A President:

Presides at all board meetings.

Makes sure that all orders and resolutions are carried out.

Signs all legal documents for the association.

Co-signs all financial documents.

Directs the activities of the association.

Sets goals that maximize association assets.

Vice President:

Substitutes for the president in his or her absence.

Secretary:

Records votes and keeps minutes of all meetings and proceedings.

Serves notices of meetings of the board and of the members.

Keeps accurate membership records.

Handles the storage, retrieval and disposal of all association documents.

Treasurer:

Receives and deposits all monies of the association.

Pays association's bills.

Signs all checks and promissory notes of the association.

Causes the annual audit or review of the books to be made.

Prepares the annual budget.

Maintains complete accounting and financial records.

Generates reports comparing actual vs. budget data.

Collects delinquent accounts.

Ensures the security of association assets.

Develops an adequate long-term replacement reserve program.

Files all tax returns.

Delivers a financial report to owners at the Annual Meeting.

---

Boards of Directors and committees, working together, create an environment of security and good communication.

Good business judgments, based on proper due diligence, result in appreciation of property values and lack of financial surprises.

---

*WHAT'S NEXT? Are management companies really necessary? The cost of professional management seems high until you understand their role.*

# SHOULD CONDOMINIUM ASSOCIATIONS HIRE PROFESSIONAL MANAGEMENT COMPANIES?

Got a question?

Got a complaint?

Got a problem?

*Call the manager!*

Hundreds of thousands of dollars are missing from 50 condominium associations across northeast Ohio. A management company and its owners are being investigated because the money the associations paid toward keeping their properties maintained is gone. The management company abruptly closed its doors, leaving employees without jobs, and the association fees for 9,000 units are now under investigation. The members of one association thought they had $146,000 in the bank, but when they actually looked at their account, they found $338. Those associations' boards are now scrambling to find new property managers and are worried about paying all their bills.

## CREDENTIALS

*There are good and bad managers!* If the association you are considering employs a management company or an on-site manager, you should <u>check out the company's or manager's credentials</u>.

There are a number of trade organizations that offer education and recognition in the form of designations to managers. Two of the most widely known are IREM, which focuses on property management professionals, and CAI, whose members include a range of industry professionals. Check whether your association's management has any of these credentials:

<u>Institute of Real Estate Management (IREM)</u>
- Certified Property Manager (CPM)
- Accredited Management Organization (AMO)

<u>Community Associations Institute (CAI)</u>
- Association Management Specialist (AMS)
- Certified Manager of Community Associations (CMCA)
- Professional Community Association Manager (PCAM)
- Accredited Association Management Company (AAMC).

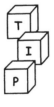

*Buyer's Tip—These designations carry weight and value. They have requirements for continuing education and adherence to strict ethical standards. Whether it's handling the association's money or recommending contractors, buyers and owners want to be assured they can trust those doing so!*

# A CONDOMINIUM MANAGEMENT COMPANY IS HIRED TO:

☺ 1. Preserve community assets

2. Maintain property values

3. Establish management continuity (board members may change annually)

4. Provide professional expertise in managing the property

5. Provide professional assistance in financial matters

6. Inform the Board of Directors about changes that occur in local, state, and federal regulations that may affect the community

# ADVANTAGES OF A MANAGEMENT COMPANY

☺ 1. Condominium purchasers are more likely to buy a unit in a professionally managed complex.

2. A lending institution will be more likely to lend money on a unit if the association employs professional management.

3. If the association employs a management company, the need for volunteer work is reduced.

4. The management company normally has a system to handle emergencies.

5. The management company should be bonded, which safeguards the association's funds.

6. When conflicts arise between owners, a third party (the management company) deals with them.

7. Management companies offer quick response to maintenance issues.

8. Projects are usually performed on a timely and cost-effective basis.

9. Costly mistakes should be minimized due to the company's knowledge and experience.

10. Access is provided to the management company's large pool of contractors.

## A MANAGEMENT COMPANY'S DUTIES INCLUDE:

☺  1. Maintaining the common elements, facilities, and equipment

2. Preparing specifications and obtain quotes for major repairs and improvements

3. Periodically inspecting and reporting on common elements and facilities

4. Collecting all assessments (maintenance fees)

5. Paying the association's invoices

6. Preparing the annual budget for the association and distribute it to all owners

7. Preparing the association's monthly financial statements for the board and maintaining financial records as required by the American Institute of Certified Public Accountants (AICPA)

8. Assisting the board with preparation of long-range plans and investment of funds

9. Supervising on-site staff

10. Handling the association's correspondence

11. Maintaining the association's files

12. Enforcing the association's governing documents

13. Ensuring the association is complying with all local laws regarding repairs and replacements

14. Answering the unit owners' questions
15. Developing and administering an effective complaint procedure
16. Communicating with prospective buyers, realtors, and mortgage institutions
17. Handling insurance matters for the property
18. Preparing and distributing meeting notices
19. Attending all meetings of the owners and Board of Directors
20. Having 24/7 emergency phone service available.

 *Buyer's Tip—The Board of Directors delegates its authority to execute these functions to the management company, but the board __always__ retains the responsibility to oversee and supervise implementation of them.*

## A MANAGEMENT COMPANY DOES NOT DO THE FOLLOWING:

1. Act as a liaison between the developer and an owner.
2. Repair an individual unit owner's property.
3. Make structural changes, alterations, or additions to common elements and facilities.
4. Advance their own funds to pay association bills.
5. Supply an audit for annual income and expenses or prepare the tax return.
6. Provide legal advice, appraisals, or brokerage services.
7. Take direction from individual owners.
8. Turn a landscape maintenance contractor into a gardener.

9. Baby-sit contractors.

10. Enforce civil and criminal law violations.

11. Act as police and enforce conduct violations.

12. Create newsletters.

13. Take meeting minutes.

14. Pay for record storage.

---

- *The relationship between the management company and the association is easily understood. They are on the same side—that of the community and its association.*
- *Running an association is a highly time-consuming job. Details must be monitored, action must be taken to solve problems, and rules must be enforced.*
- *Even though management companies are external third parties, they perform an internal support role, and they have the benefit of objectivity. They are the operational arm for the community.*

# GLOSSARY

**Ad Hoc Committee**   Committee that is appointed to carry out a specific task and is disbanded when that task is completed.

**Agent for Service of Process**   Person or firm named in the Articles of Incorporation who receives all legal notices on behalf of the association, usually referred to as the Statutory Agent.

**Alternative Dispute Resolution (ADR)**   Methods of resolving disputes, including mediation and arbitration, other than by judicial process.

**Amendment**   Revision of a governing document.

**Annual Meeting**   Once-a-year assemblage of unit owners required by the governing documents to conduct association business (such as electing a Board of Directors).

**Articles of Incorporation**   Formal document that sets up an association as a corporation under the laws of the applicable state when it is filed. It also describes the purpose, powers, and duties of the association.

**Assessments**   Amounts charged against unit owners (according to their percentages of ownership) to fund the operation, administration, maintenance, and management of the community association.

**Association**   *See* Community Association.

**Audit**    Examination of inventories, insurance policies, management, and financial records and accounts to verify their accuracy and determine if they adequately reflect an association's financial status.

**Balance Sheet**    The financial statement that indicates the financial status of an association at a specific time, listing its assets, liabilities, and members' equity.

**Board**    *See* Board of Directors.

**Board Meetings**    Any gathering of at least a quorum of the Board of Directors for the purpose of transacting the business of the association.

**Board of Directors**    Official governing body that is responsible for administration of the association. The Board of Directors is elected by the members of the association.

**Breach of Covenants**    Non-compliance with the governing documents of the association.

**Budget**    Estimated summary of income and expenses for a given period.

**Bundle of Rights**    The bundle of rights is defined in the deed to the property and typically contains all of the rights of ownership originally connected to that parcel. In a condominium association, the Declaration defines these rights.

**Bylaws**    Secondary laws of an association that govern its internal affairs and deal with routine operational and administrative matters.

**Capital Expenditures**    Funds spent for additions or improvements to the common elements and facilities of the association.

**Casualty Insurance**    *See* Liability Insurance.

**Certified Public Accountant (CPA)**    An accountant who has met certain state legal requirements.

**Chain of Title**   *See* Bundle of Rights.

**Common Areas**   *See* Common Elements & Facilities.

**Common Elements & Facilities**   Property owned jointly by all unit owners, that ordinarily includes land and structures not otherwise described as units.

**Common Expenses**   Costs of managing, maintaining, administering, repairing, replacing, and operating the association.

**Community Association**   Private organization, usually nonprofit, responsible for the total operation of communities such as condominiums, homeowner associations, and cooperatives. The individual owners are members of the association.

**Condominium**   Form of ownership in a multi-family housing association that combines exclusive ownership of a dwelling unit and joint ownership of common elements and facilities.

**Conflict of Interest**   Situation in which a person has two or more interests that conflict.

**Declarant**   The person or company who creates and files the governing documents and then develops and sells the condominium association property.

**Declarant Expansion Period**   The period of time, beyond the initial creation, that the Declarant has to add land, units, and other improvements to the condominium association.

**Declaration**   *See* Declaration of Condominium Ownership.

**Declaration of Condominium Ownership**   The basic document recorded at a government office to set out property interests in a community association. It also describes each unit owner's undivided share in the common elements and facilities and restrictions on the use of the units and common elements and facilities.

**Delinquency**   Overdue assessment payment.

**Developer**   *See* Declarant.

**Directors & Officers Liability Insurance**   Protection against loss arising out of errors in judgment, breaches of duty and wrongful acts of a Board of Directors and officers in carrying out their prescribed duties.

**Disclosure Package**   A summary of the significant features of the condominium as well as the governing documents. This is the package normally presented to prospective buyers by the Declarant prior to binding the sale agreement.

**Easement**   Right to use or enter property by someone other than the owner for certain limited purposes.

**Escrow Fee**   An extra fee charged at the closing of a sale for rendering information on the status of the unit's account, association's insurance coverage, closing confirmation of the account, and processing of the unit owner's record changes. This fee is charged by the association or management company, normally to the seller.

**Exclusive Use Areas**   Parts of the condominium's common elements and facilities that owners have the right to use and enjoy privately, such as patios.

**Executive Session**   Meeting of the Board of Directors that owners are not permitted to attend.

**Fiduciary Duty**   This duty requires the Board of Directors to act for the benefit of the community as a whole. It is the Board's legal obligation to protect the asset, which is the total community.

**First Right of Refusal**   A right that may be held by the association that gives it the first option to buy a unit that is being sold.

**Fiscal Year**   Twelve-month period for which an association plans the use of funds.

**Foreclosure**   The taking away of the right of ownership of a condominium unit in order to pay the delinquency owed to the association.

**Governing Documents**   Set of legal papers, filed by a declarant at the appropriate local land office, that submits land to use for, create, and govern a community association.

**Homeowners' Association**   Organization of homeowners whose major purpose is to maintain and provide for the rights of owners and maintenance of the common elements and facilities.

**Indemnification**   Condition, usually contractual, of being protected against possible damage, loss, or lawsuit.

**Insurance**   Protective measure that shifts risk of financial loss, due to certain perils, to an insurance company in return for payment of premiums.

**Liability Insurance**   Coverage for damages arising out of an insured person's legal responsibility and resulting from injuries to other persons or damage to their property.

**Lien**   Claim or attachment, enforceable by law, to have a debt or other charge satisfied out of a person's property.

**Limited Common Areas**   *See* Limited Common Elements & Facilities.

**Limited Common Elements & Facilities**   Physical part of a community association's common elements that is reserved for the exclusive use of a particular unit owner or owners.

**Maintenance Fees**   *See* Assessments.

**Majority Vote**   Simple majority vote is fifty-one percent (51%) of the owners or the Board of Directors.

**Management Company**   Firm that specialized in community association management, hired by the association to carry out the board's policies and provide the day-to-day operation of the affairs of the association.

**Mandatory Committee**   Group of people formed to handle ongoing business on a certain subject, as required in the Bylaws.

**Master Deed**   Recorded instrument that describes the property involved in a community association.

**Minutes**   Official record of the proceedings of a meeting.

**Newsletter**   Printed periodical report devoted to news of and for the association members and others associated with the community.

**Operating Budget**   Portion of the budget that indicates the expenses of operation for the association, other than the replacement funds.

**Order of Business**   Formal guidelines for conducting a business meeting, usually Robert's Rules of Order.

**Organizational Meeting**   Meeting of the Board of Directors at which they elect the officers of the board.

**Percentage of Interest**   *See* Percentage of Ownership.

**Percentage of Ownership**   The ownership share in the common elements and facilities that is assigned to each unit by the Declarant in the Declaration. The percentage for each unit sharing the common expenses must be the same as the ownership share for the unit. The total percentage of all units must equal 100.

**Phase Condominium**   A single association created over time by the Declarant. New units are added to the project by amending the Declaration, thus changing the percentages of ownership as they are added.

**Plat**   A drawing that is recorded in the local land records office before any units are sold. Its purpose is to show the precise location of each unit, as well as the common elements, and define the owner's and the community's title to the property.

**Profit & Loss Statement** *See* Statement of Income & Expense.

**Property Insurance** Protection of an insured person's real or personal property against loss or damage.

**Proxy** Authorization given to one person to vote in place of another at an association meeting.

**Quorum** Minimum number of members that must be present or votes that must be represented in or order for business to be legally transacted.

**Regulations** *See* Rules.

**Replacement Expenses** Costs to repair and replace existing property with property of the same material and construction.

**Replacement Fund** Funds that are restricted and set aside for probable repair and replacement of common elements and facilities at some future time. These funds should be in an account separate from the operating funds.

**Reserve Fund** *See* Replacement Fund.

**Reserve Study** Document prepared periodically by or for the association documenting the physical condition of the property that it is obligated to monitor, the funds allocated for its upkeep and maintenance, and the forecasted annual use of those funds.

**Resolutions** *See* Rules.

**Rules** Statements of required, specific behavior whose violation carries a penalty. Rules generally cover the use of and changes to the architecture or appearance of the property, as well as behavior of the residents.

**Special Assessment** Fee levied against unit owners to cover unexpected expenses.

**Special Meeting** Unscheduled meeting called by the Board of Directors or owners to discuss specific, urgent business.

**Statement of Income & Expense**   Financial report that
indicates how much income has been earned and what
expenses have been paid over a certain period of time.
This statement also usually compares budgeted and actual
figures for the period in question and year to date.

**Undivided Interest**   The percentage of ownership in the
common elements and facilities that is attached to a unit.
This share passes with title to a unit and cannot be
separated.

**Unit**   Part of the condominium property that is subject to
exclusive ownership. The definition is specified in the
Declaration.

**Unit Owners Association**   *See* Association.

**Voting Rights**   Authorization given to each unit owner to
choose a specific course of action or elect a board member.
Owners have either one vote per unit or vote according to
their percentage of ownership in their unit according to
the Declaration and/or Bylaws.

# Index

Made in the USA
San Bernardino, CA
16 November 2012